FLIGHT TO FREEDOM

THE STORY OF THE UNDERGROUND RAILROAD

by Henrietta Buckmaster

FLIGHT TO
FREEDOM

THE STORY OF THE
UNDERGROUND RAILROAD

Thomas Y. Crowell Company
New York

Manufactured in the United States of America by the
Vail-Ballou Press, Inc., Binghamton, New York
Library of Congress Catalog Card No. 58-9731
Sixth Printing

For Nancy
with my love

I

ONE hot day in 1850, a man staggered out of a woods, looked about him to get his bearings, and plunged down a lane toward the river. He had only a few moments of freedom before he heard the baying of hounds. But those few minutes were all he needed to splash up to his knees in the shallow stream and wade, half crouching, under the willow trees, then turn swiftly in the opposite direction. At length he submerged himself in the water, breathing through a hollow reed he held in his hand.

The dogs tried desperately to pick up the scent but the water had destroyed it. Since the man had created a false scent before doubling back on his tracks, the shouting men and the milling dogs raced up the stream in the opposite direction.

After a safe interval, the man scrambled up the bank and sat panting and shaking with nerves. He knew he had no time to waste. It was growing dark, and the darkness would help him. He waded across the stream and ran, crouching, through the cotton fields until he reached a footpath.

The only guide he had was the North Star. The only friend he could trust in the whole world was himself. Yet his skin was black and this fact might betray him. The man was a fugitive slave and the entire law was arrayed against him. The roads were patrolled by armed men on horseback who kept a watch for such as he. Patrols shot first and asked questions second.

The North Star was his hope . . . north . . . keep going north and eventually, if you do not die, you will find freedom.

The man had had the nails of one foot torn out because he had tried to run away before. The toes ached now but he scarcely felt the pain. All night he stumbled through underbrush, ran along the side of the road. When he saw the first light of dawn, he drew some water from a well. Before he could lower the bucket again, a voice whispered, *What you doing here? What you want?*

For answer, he struck out his fist, not even waiting to learn whether the questioner was white or Negro. *Wait— you're a fool!* the voice said more urgently. *You can't get away in the daytime. Lay over. I'll get you some breakfast.*

The voice belonged to a black man. Those two who crouched by the well, looking at each other, were both slaves. They understood without further words.

The runaway—we'll call him Jeb—spent the day hidden in an unused pigpen in the woods. He ate and slept.

2

At night, his friend brought him some sow back and corn bread and showed him a short cut through the woods. He could not tell Jeb how far he was from the "North." Only Jeb's torn and exhausted feet and his fear could give him any sense of the distance.

For another ten days Jeb lived in deadly danger. He existed as best he could. He once ate poisonous berries and nearly died, with no one to help. The next day he crept on a bare two miles, but he was not defeated.

His pants were torn, his shirt was frayed. A slave gave him a better pair of pants. A woman flung him a coat. A white woman. . . . Another white woman saw him in a field, ducking down behind a wall. She had in her hand a bowl of table scraps for the chickens. She put the bowl on the wall and called softly, "Come and get it."

A slave told him he was in Kentucky, close to the Ohio River. He almost fainted. Get across that river, and he'd be in the Promised Land—almost. *Swim,* his black friend told him. *Ain't hard. Fix to cross over at Ripley and you'll see a light burning on a hill. That's friends. You won't have to worry no more.*

Jeb came to the river at twilight. Nothing ever looked so wide or so wet. Hiding in bushes, he stared at the river and then he lifted his eyes to the hills. He continued to stare at the hills. With the first darkness, a light flickered high on the crest of the hill. A friend or a decoy? He took the risk and slipped into the water.

For a man who was weak and exhausted it was a hard swim. When he climbed out on the other bank he did not know whether he would be able to climb that hill. Over and over he repeated to himself: *freedom—freedom—freedom*. It was the most beautiful sound in the world.

In the state of Ohio were no slave whips, no slave shackles, no slave men. It gave Jeb strength. He climbed the steep road, and he stood for a moment by the garden gate looking south across that flowing river. He'd never go back.

The family who lived beyond the garden gate was named Rankin. Seven tall sons and a father were prepared at any time of the day or night to pass along a runaway.

They passed this one along. But first they gave Jeb a meal, made him a bed of straw in the bottom of a wagon, and then, in the dead of night, a Rankin son hitched up the team and drove through the rutty darkness to the home of a friend.

The friend was unsurprised and prepared. Since it was now nearly dawn, he hid Jeb in his barn, but that night he hitched up *his* team and drove Jeb another thirty miles. In Canada lay the only true safety, for slave masters and slave laws could reach into the North with a long arm. Five more days of hazard and hardship, of tenderness, care, and brotherly love, and then the wide expanse of Lake Erie danced in the sunlight. Jeb was smuggled aboard a ship and hidden under sacks of grain. When he stepped off the ship, he was a free man.

This was the desire for freedom which sent more than two thousand slaves out of the South every year. This was the Underground Railroad.

Slavery had lain like a terrible sore on our country for

two hundred years. Many were ashamed of it. The black Africans who were enslaved fought against it from the start. Men like Thomas Jefferson, preparing the Declaration of Independence and the Constitution, tried to have slavery outlawed. It was well on its way to extinction when a machine was invented in the late eighteenth century. The cotton gin. This machine cleaned five hundred pounds of cotton a day instead of the five that a man could do by hand. To grow the cotton to feed the machine, plantation owners needed labor—cheap labor. That settled the fate of slavery. To abolish slavery meant to abolish profits which were astronomical, profits which were shared North and South.

But *not* to abolish slavery struck at some of the deepest principles of Americans. For the next sixty years—until the crash of the Civil War—no issue was as important as slavery. It divided homes, it spoke for the conscience, it made political parties, it challenged religion, it turned men into brutes and it turned men into heroes. It created the Underground Railroad.

The first slave who helped a fellow slave to escape drove the first spike in this invisible railroad. The unknown first fugitive, the softly stepping men and women who dared the dangers of swamps and mountains and of cold and rain, the outstretched hands of friends, the disguises, the courage, the gunshots along the border, and a long invisible "train" which chugged so silently and sent up such invisible smoke—all these proved in the end irresistible. It was they which really broke the chains of slavery.

2.

"CHAINS of slavery" is the right phrase.

No one was free and independent where slavery existed.

There were eleven million people in the South. Of these only three hundred fifty thousand held slaves. The rest—four million Negroes and more than six and a half million slaveless whites—were chained to slavery: the Negroes were owned body and soul, the slaveless whites were bound economically, as we shall see.

Almost all the six and a half million slaveless whites were desperately poor and could do little to change their condition. The reason for this lay in the psychology of slavery.

Factories and industry, where men might have taken jobs, were practically nonexistent in the South. Cotton ruled everything. The poor white had no way in which to

6

buy the large tracts of land which alone made the growing of cotton economical.

With the exception of some rice growing along the sea coast, cotton was the only large crop of the South. Yet cotton wears out the soil quicker than almost any other crop. Only the large plantations could afford to let some of their land lie fallow and still have a large enough crop for profit. If the poor white tried growing small patches of cotton (and he persistently did), he was in hopeless competition with the big cotton growers.

Any serious efforts to introduce new crops and rotate them with cotton ran into such determined opposition from the large planters that they came to nothing.

Politically and socially and morally, the three hundred fifty thousand slaveowners dominated the South. Southern churches preached regular sermons saying that God approved of slavery. Southern newspapers printed nothing unfriendly to slavery. Southern legislators took great care that only laws favorable to slavery were passed.

It was a vicious circle.

In an economy that depended on debased and enslaved labor, a white man could not work with his hands, in the fields, for another white man, and not assume in his own mind and in the mind of his employer some of the attributes of a slave. This was, of course, nonsense, but a nonsense that was believed in devoutly. Because of this, even overseers—so indispensable on a large plantation—were usually drawn from Northerners or from the lowliest white groups of the South.

Just before the Civil War, a book created a tremendous

stir and became famous. It was called *The Impending Crisis in the South* and was written by a nonslaveholding North Carolina man named H. R. Helper. This is what he said, and it is worth reading carefully because few denied its correctness at the time it appeared.

For the last sixty years, slaveholders have been the constant representatives of the South, and what have they accomplished? We . . . point to our thinly inhabited states, to our fields, stripped of their virgin soil, to the despicable price of lands, to our unvisited cities and towns, to our vacant harbors and idle water power, to the dreary absence of shipping and manufactures, to the millions of living monuments of ignorance, to the squalid poverty of the whites, and to the utter wretchedness of the blacks. . . . Notwithstanding the fact that the nonslaveholders of the South are in the majority, six to one, they have never yet had an uncontrolled part in framing the laws under which they live. There is no legislation except for the benefit of slavery and slaveholders. As a general rule, poor white persons are regarded with less esteem and attention than Negroes, and though the condition of the latter is wretched beyond description, vast numbers of the former are infinitely worse off. To all intents and purposes, they are disfranchised and outlawed, and the only privilege extended is a narrow and circumscribed participation in the political movements that usher slaveholders into office.

Helper created a sensation. He had to escape from North Carolina before a lynch mob, but his facts were never seriously disputed.

8

None of these events happened overnight. The first chain had been fastened by the invention of the cotton gin, and the final chains by the invention, in England, of a spinning machine and a weaving machine that made cotton goods cheaply available to the whole world.

All the cotton that the South could produce was fed into these machines—and to similar machines in the North—and thus brought prosperity to a great many men. Cheap labor for picking, ginning, baling, and transporting cotton was now essential; and the cheapest labor of all was the slave.

There was nothing wrong about prosperity for the South! All that was wrong was the assumption that slave labor produced it more effectively. Eventually the North, with its industrial development and waves of immigration, was to prove to the South that its way to prosperity was better in every sense of the word. When this happened, the two sections of the country stood on the edge of Civil War.

Slavery was not chained to the country without many protests. When our Constitution was being prepared, men like Benjamin Franklin, Patrick Henry, and Thomas Jefferson did all they could to include a denunciation of slavery. In the end, they were obliged to compromise on something more general . . . "We hold these truths to be self-evident, that all men are created equal, that they are endowed by their Creator with certain unalienable Rights, that among these are Life, Liberty and the pursuit of Happiness." *All men* . . . .

In addition, they wrote into the Constitution a ruling

that by 1807 the slave trade should come to an end. But when 1807 arrived, cotton planters did not want their supply of cheap labor cut off.

A simple way around the constitutional requirement was found: the law forbidding the slave trade was passed and promptly forgotten. Slave smuggling became so profitable that the master of a slave ship, sailing the Atlantic from Africa to the United States, could permit nine slaves out of ten to die from neglect and still lose no money.

Humane men were deeply shocked. They protested, and then they did more than protest—they helped the Negro.

A large number of these men and women were Quakers, or people with a religious conviction that slavery was against the will of God. They found that the slave had been protesting for many long years and all they had to do was to hold out a hand and a runaway would grasp it.

Negroes had been showing their contempt for slavery from the first moment they landed in America. In 1526, when Spanish explorers landed with Negro slaves in what is now South Carolina, the first armed Negro uprising took place. The newspapers and the law courts of the South showed that over two hundred revolts and uprisings, carefully planned and carried out by slaves, took place in the eighteenth and nineteenth centuries. And the runaways' line of escape ran its winding course through every state from Alabama to the Canadian border.

These escape routes were well chosen for practical reasons. The first goal in most cases was either Ohio or Pennsylvania. Those slaves from the Deep South, who could stow away on a Mississippi River boat, might, with good luck, find themselves on the Ohio River. Ohio had been settled by New Englanders in the northern part and by Southerners in the southern part. But many of these Southerners were men and women who had left their homes because they hated slavery, and the fugitive found helpers at almost any point along the shore.

As we have seen with our friend Jeb, he would be passed from house to house until—in the early days—he reached the wilderness of central and western Ohio where the Ottawa Indians gave him assistance. From there he could be sent into the Western Reserve where the pioneer town of Hudson, Ohio, was being made into a solid antislavery stronghold by men like Owen Brown and his son, John. Or he might go through the Firelands, in northwestern Ohio, where men were willing to dare anything for a fugitive.

All the routes led to the Great Lakes, and the final task was to conceal the runaway on a sailing boat or send him by way of Buffalo and Niagara into Canada.

Next in importance to Ohio—or perhaps equal to it— was Pennsylvania, and runaways coming from Virginia and North Carolina found in the Quakers quick and ready friends who would hurry them into the northwest tip of the state from which the final plunge could be taken.

Whether the escape route lay through Ohio or Pennsylvania—or Indiana or New England—the goal was Canada.

It is true that many fugitives went no farther than New York or Boston, where they got work and settled down to live as free men, but there was no real safety south of the Canadian border.

Canada was no haven of milk and honey. The Negro suffered hardships that must have made him often wonder whether he had merely exchanged one wretched life for another. A cruel climate, a desolate wilderness from which homes must be wrung, loneliness—yet so few returned to the warm and cozy land of slavery that a return was a matter of open-mouthed amazement. In Canada, in spite of physical sufferings, the Negro found safety, opportunity, and self-respect.

The men and women who helped the runaway slave knew the risks they were taking. They knew that they had to do everything humanly possible to make sure that no escape failed. The risks were very great, for in 1793 a Fugitive Slave Law had been passed which put the fugitive at the mercy of any circuit judge or state magistrate, who could decide, on whatever evidence he chose, to send him back to slavery. The law also fined anyone who hid a runaway five hundred dollars.

For the sake of both slave and friend, an escape had to be successful. It was a miracle how often escapes did succeed.

To the Quakers, breaking the law was a grievous matter. In order to quiet their conscience, they often juggled

12

with the truth. The letter of the law was never broken by them, but it found itself in many strange shapes.

John and Mary Smith, for example (Quakers in the southern part of Pennsylvania), showed how such a problem could be handled.

Two women fugitives appealed to them for protection. The slave catcher was close behind them, and not a moment could be lost. Without a word, Mary drew the women into the house and John stationed himself by the door. Taking the women into the bedroom, Mary lifted the mattress off the bed and told them to lie flat on the ropes. She then replaced the mattress, made up the bed again, and smoothed the counterpane so that not a wrinkle betrayed a hiding place.

John, meanwhile, was having a hard time to control not only his temper but the slave catchers who were demanding the right to search the house. His Quaker principles of nonresistance were being put to a hard test when his wife appeared in the doorway and said, "Let them come in, John. Thee knows there are no slaves here."

She spoke the truth. To the Quaker, no such creature as a slave existed.

White friends had to assume that a fugitive had no other helper in the world and had to bear as full a responsibility as the occasion demanded.

When Hannah Gibbons, who was also a Quaker, took a weary, sick, and filthy fugitive into her house, she obeyed this sense of Christian love. When he soon fell sick of smallpox, she nursed him for six weeks as tenderly as she would her son. To women like Hannah Gibbons, this was loving one's neighbor.

Bit by bit, the friends of the runaway found that their own usefulness was in proportion to their quick-wittedness. In nine times out of ten, this meant, "Find a loophole in the law!" So, when a devoted antislavery lawyer applied himself to a study of state laws, uncanny results followed, and loopholes appeared as though by magic.

Isaac Tatum Hopper was a perfect example of one of these lawyer-friends. For a man such as he, nothing was too daring. He had imagination, resourcefulness, courage, and a sense of humor. He lived in Philadelphia at the turn of the nineteenth century.

Philadelphia was the prowling place of the agents of the slave masters. Fugitives, and free Negroes, were frequently seized by these men and carried, bound, over the state border as fast as possible. These outrages became the special concern of Friend Hopper. Eventually he became such a master of the loophole that a slaveowner would rather deal with the devil than with Hopper.

On one occasion he was wakened early in the morning and told by a Negro friend that a fugitive had been recaptured by the master and was to be sent out of the state as fast as possible. Hopper dressed hurriedly and ran all the way to the tavern where the fugitive was being held. He pushed aside the landlord, who tried to prevent his entrance, and ran up the stairs to the room where the captive was held. He found the slave bound to a chair and guarded by six men.

"What are you doing with this man?" he cried almost before he had the door open.

The answer fell on him like an avalanche. In less time than he had taken to climb the stairs he was flying through the open window. He said later that he was so determined on rescue that he hardly knew what happened to him. His clothes were torn, his body ached; but, even while his attackers were congratulating themselves on the way they had finished him off forever, he rushed around to the front door and darted once more up the stairs.

The door was locked. With time pressing so urgently, he ran to the yard again, climbed to the roof of a shed by means of a high board fence, and forced his way into the adjoining room.

His jackknife sprang open as he confronted the slave catchers. He cried, "Let me see if you will get me out so soon again!" as he cut the ropes that bound the slave. Shouting, "Follow me!" he opened the door and dashed down the stairs as fast as he could.

The slave was almost as quick as he, but the astonishment of the slave catchers made them slow to take action. By the time they had gathered themselves together, Hopper and the slave were halfway down the street. The slave catchers joined a crowd, which had quickly formed, and chased the two men for half a mile, shouting "Stop thief!"

However, Hopper knew where he was running and the others did not. *He* was heading for the office of a justice of the peace. He was heading straight for a loophole.

The justice, with an amazement almost equal to the slave catchers', looked at the bleeding and disheveled Quaker who pushed the slave in before him and slammed the door.

"Good heavens, Mr. Hopper!" he cried, "what brings you here this time of the morning in such a trim and with such a rabble at your heels?"

Mr. Hopper explained the situation in a few well-chosen words, and the judge burst out laughing: "They don't know you as well as we do, Friend Hopper!" And he agreed to a legal maneuver that protected the fugitive.

Isaac Hopper depended on Pennsylvania justice, and it seldom failed him. If the worst came to the worst, he could—by one means or another—keep the case of a fugitive in the courts for three or four years. By that time the claimants were sick to death of it and willing to make any settlement. The law possessed an elemental clarity until submitted to the benign scrutiny of Mr. Hopper. Then it became a plagued instrument, designed exclusively to outwit slaveowners.

3

THIS should be the right place—before we go deeper into the dangers and drama of the Underground Railroad—to get rid of a large amount of misinformation. Unless we do so, it will be hard to understand properly the intense and wonderful excitement of that "underground road."

First and foremost: the Negro had not always been a slave. In his own continent, Africa, there had been ancient civilizations which were highly developed when the European was still a barbarian.

Certain Pharaohs of Egypt had been mulatto—half Negro, half white. Negro empires had stretched across the continent from coast to coast. Black Africans were the first to discover the smelting of iron. In some of their coastal cities they had universities.

17

They were painters, sculptors, and textile weavers. They were explorers. Balboa found Negroes among the Indians of Darien. Perhaps they were descendants of those African voyagers who were said to have come to the New World before Columbus.

African empires began to break apart when the Persians, the Romans, the Byzantines cast envious glances toward Africa. The black Africans fought them all; they fought among themselves. This weakened them so much that, when the first Moslem slave traders came from the east in the fourteenth century, and the first Christian slave traders from the west in the fifteenth, the Africans could not resist.

The slave traders made and unmade tribal kings, they stirred up wars among the Negroes and bought the captives. They even set fire to native villages and captured the inhabitants as they ran to safety. Between the Moslems and the Christians, one hundred million Africans were taken from their homes over a period of three hundred years and sold into slavery.

The first African slave arrived in English America in 1619. But one fact is not generally known: many of the Africans who were later brought here were not slaves. A surprising number came as indentured servants—just as did many white men.

An indentured servant was a free man who bound himself to work a specified number of years for a master who agreed to provide his board and keep. In the seven, or ten, years of indenture, he would help his master to build up the farm or plantation (or business) and, at the end of that time, go his own way or enter into a new contract of additional servitude. No capital investment was required of the master.

But as the economy of the South became slowly dominated by cotton, the value of the Negro, who could work long hours under the Southern sun, grew so great that the indenture system gradually became an anachronism, and means were found to enslave the Negro for life. Occasional masters in their wills freed their slaves. Occasional masters went further than that, and freed their slaves in their lifetimes. But both instances were rare, and eventually most slave states passed laws making manumission —as freedom granted by a master was called—illegal.

When the Revolution began, slaves ran away by the score to fight with the British, who promised them freedom. Thomas Jefferson said that Virginia alone lost thirty thousand slaves in this manner. In the North (which also had slavery at this time) freedom was promised to those black men who fought side by side with their masters.

But when the Revolution had been won, many masters broke their promises. The epidemic of re-enslavement was so serious that the legislature of Virginia passed an act guaranteeing freedom to those Negro soldiers who had been promised it.

Year by year, however, the laws became more cruel. Eventually a slave had no social or civil rights of any kind, and the free Southern Negro, caught in the same trap, was left with only the right to marry and to hold

19

property. Yet at one time, in the seventeenth and part of the eighteenth centuries, many black men had voted, in both the South and the North. By the end of the eighteenth century, the slave could not move off his master's land without a pass, he could not legally marry, he had no authority over his children. Families were torn apart.

Many people have tried to justify slavery by asserting that the Negro was, somehow, inferior. But history shows he was in no way inferior. Others have written stories and poems about the slaves singing at their work around a great plantation house. It is true that house slaves were often happy and devoted, but they were a small minority. The vast majority—90 per cent—were field slaves who lived an overworked and hopeless life.

It is also quite true that laws were on the statute books protecting slaves from cruelty, hunger, and neglect. But each plantation was a greater law to itself. Whether a state law was obeyed or disobeyed depended on the humanity of the masters or the overseers.

As the great plantations moved from the worn-out soil of Georgia, South Carolina, Virginia, out to the new lands of Alabama, Mississippi, and Louisiana, the majority of the owners preferred to live in the more comfortable environment of cities, and so the overseers ruled like kings.

The sole function of these enormous plantations was to produce cotton and more cotton. Living conditions were rough, comfort at a minimum. These were not places for wives and families. So the owner of a Mississippi plantation might live with his family in Natchez or Charleston or Philadelphia. The owner of a Louisiana plantation in New Orleans or New York. His visits to the huge "factories in the fields" were infrequent; and, nine times out of ten, he knew only what the overseer chose to tell. Pierce Butler, for example, who was said to own the largest number of slaves in the South, made his home in Philadelphia, and visited his Sea Islands plantations, off the coast of Georgia, once or, at the most, twice a year. Only once did he take his English wife with him, and she was so shocked by what she saw that she wrote a book called *Journal of a Residence on a Georgian Plantation,* which became a famous book during the Civil War.

On the smaller, more old-fashioned plantations there were many kind masters—or, especially, kind mistresses —who did not work their slaves unduly, who cared for them in sickness, who saw that they were clothed and fed properly, who felt an affection for certain individuals and made their old age as comfortable as possible. Jefferson Davis set up a form of self-government on his plantation and dismissed overseers who were cruel, and Robert E. Lee gave his slaves their freedom.

But such masters were rare, and even they would have been confused and troubled if you had said to them that the Negro deserved the same rights and opportunities as themselves. And they were dismayed when the Negro claimed those rights for himself by his perpetual fight against slavery.

21

According to newspapers and records of Southern law courts, over two hundred uprisings took place in the 250 years of American slavery. Slaves stole arms. They refused to work. They kept the South in a state of real or imagined ferment. They ran away, and by running away they caught the imagination of the whole world.

Some fugitives did not even attempt to come North. They lived in woods or mountains as outlaws, in bayous or swamps. The Dismal Swamp of Virginia, with its hundreds of acres, was the home of runaways for two or three generations. The Everglades of Florida drew in hundreds who lived with the Indians. They were called "maroons" and lived by hunting, fishing, or stealing food; they lived in caves or built cabins.

As time went on, and the Northern states, one by one, abolished slavery, word spread to the South that if you followed the North Star far enough you would be a free man. After the War of 1812, Southern white soldiers, returning to their homes, made a great story of the Negroes who fought in the Canadian ranks. This was enough to say that Canada was a land of freedom, and Canada then became a star of hope. Songs were sung to this Promised Land.

Some people claim that 1804 saw the "formal" beginning of the underground line. That year, in the Pennsylvania village of Columbia, certain white people were so roused by a slave agent's cruelty to a fugitive that they banded together to rescue the slave. But the underground line never had an official opening. It began when the first fugitive met his first friend. With the years it became more important, that is all. In time, this invisible "railroad" became so powerful that it chugged through the most influential parlors of the United States.

By 1818 friends in Pennsylvania and Ohio knew which routes of escape were the safest, knew that the fellow up the pike in the red farmhouse could be relied on, knew that that fellow in the next township with the silky manners could not be trusted with last year's bag of oats —knew, above all, that their own imagination and quick wits were more important than any amount of disguise.

Disguises were not overlooked, of course, but these depended on the emergency of the moment. It is hard to disguise a black skin, but often a Negro man was dressed in widow's weeds, with a heavy black veil concealing his face, and driven safely in an open carriage to the next hiding place. Or a young Negro woman would have her hair clipped short like a boy's, be given men's clothes, and set on her way disguised as a carpenter or a bricklayer.

Secrecy, and a carefully encouraged mystery, was the strength of the Underground Railroad. It grew like a vine in all directions. From one successful escape grew fifty more. From one failure grew greater determination to succeed the next time.

Every slave cabin knew about the mysterious "glory road" that could sweep the slave out into freedom. Every Negro church in the slave South learned to speak a disguised language about the "sweet chariot" that was "going to carry me home."

Not every slave dared think of mounting that heavenly chariot, but he talked about it, and he helped others to climb aboard. And any slave who had a pipeline to a free Negro kept it open, for the free Negro stood just at that borderline of night and day: he could see in two directions, he was on speaking terms with the "chariot," he knew the lingo of the underground line.

Although free Negroes were a mere handful in the South, in the North they were legion. They were the eyes and ears, the quick fingers, the very heartbeat of freedom. Without them, many of the white friends of the fugitive would have been helpless, not knowing where and how to help. In addition, the white man saw, in the independence and self-respect and industry of the free Negro, proof that the black man was his equal.

This proof could make all the difference between life and death, escape or failure, for many white people needed persuasion. They did not want their lives disturbed. They did not want their consciences roused. The free Negro was a perpetual reminder that slavery was a sickening thing.

When a free Negro brought an exhausted fugitive to a white man's house after dark and begged for assistance, he was asking help in the name of human decency. When the free Negro was himself kidnaped and sold into slavery —and this happened with a dreadful frequency—his cry was the cry of all humanity. Only men made of stone could resist.

And men were not made of stone. They reached out their hands.

Thus friends began to smooth the rutty road to freedom, friends who were strong enough to protect the fugitive, friends who would grow with the next sixty years, lie for them, pass laws to protect them, go to prison for them, be put out of the church for them, die for them. And, above all, see nothing strange in working side by side with Negroes to create a common purpose out of the confusions and dreams of a new country.

4

IT was these same friends—people with humanity in their hearts—who first heard Benjamin Lundy in 1815. This little Quaker, Lundy, was a kind of wandering saint. With him, a new and powerful force began slowly to be felt.

He made the suffering of the slave his own suffering. With no money he started a small newspaper with a huge name: *The Genius of Universal Emancipation.*

He lived in Ohio, and the only available press was in Mount Pleasant, twenty miles from his home. When he went to the press he walked those twenty miles and back again. The first issue was bought by six people. Within half a year, the subscribers increased to five hundred, and with this encouragement he determined to carry the word far and wide.

Traveling mostly by foot, a knapsack on his back, he cried out his message against slavery wherever people gathered. Wherever he found a friendly printer, he stopped long enough to print a new issue of *The Genius of Universal Emancipation.*

In ten years he traveled twenty five thousand miles. Five thousand of them were on foot. His brother, the colored man, was his life. He went to Canada to see for himself the condition of the fugitives. Twice he went through the wild Mexican province of Texas into Mexico itself, seeking a grant of land which fugitives might call their own. He suffered from hunger, thirst, and exposure, but he was sustained by a conviction and a burning zeal.

His accomplishments were small, his scope was limited, but he represented with a homely grandeur the love of justice which makes a great man. He knew that every voice raised in protest, every effort to draw together a shield of friends, forged a strong and sturdy cooperation between the two races.

The pattern of abolition was beginning to take shape. *Abolition* was a step beyond *antislavery*. It was a positive and active effort to abolish slavery immediately, in contrast to the philosophy of antislavery, which merely opposed, and was content to wait for the future to take care of the problem of enslavement.

Little Lundy, wandering up and down the country, was helping to strengthen abolition. Yet how weak and pointless he must have seemed before the great might of slavery. For the slave power possessed everything. It almost drew Illinois into the orbit of slavery. It got Missouri.

The Missouri Compromise belongs to our school books. Sufficient to say, it was a compromise whereby all states, in the future, would be admitted to the Union in pairs, one slave, one free. In addition, it gave to the South the right to capture their fugitives in territories north of the compromise line. John Quincy Adams called it bitterly "the title page of a great tragic volume."

Abolitionists replied to the Missouri Compromise by increasing their efforts. New havens on the underground line opened by the dozen. So successful were the abolitionists that Kentucky and Maryland begged Congress, again and again, to take action against these enemies of the slave catcher.

Such turbulent and uneasy times were preparing for even more turbulent and uneasy times. In 1821, Denmark Vesey, a free Negro of Charleston, South Carolina, attempted a greater overturning of the slave power than had yet been dreamed of in the United States.

Vesey read the Bible and spoke in Old Testament terms against "the oppressors." He read smuggled antislavery pamphlets and anything else that fed his hatred of slavery. He knew that the Missouri Compromise had extended the power of slavery, and he hated those who had given slavery this added strength. He was a handsome man with a powerful personality, and he was accepted as a natural leader. In the words of one of his friends, "If a colored man bowed to a white person he would rebuke him, and observe that all men were born equal, and that he was surprised that anyone would degrade himself by such conduct."

He planned an uprising with such care that not even a rumor escaped. For their meetings he and his friends chose a farm that could be reached by water and would enable them to avoid the patrols which kept a watch for slaves without passes—that written permission to travel even a few miles, which every slave had to carry. They made their own weapons and recruited slaves from all the plantations about. The number of recruits reached the thousands—six thousand, some said, nine thousand according to others. After the betrayal of their plans, the leaders conducted themselves so calmly that their jailers were deceived and released them.

But they were soon rearrested—130 of them—and the revenge was sweeping. Only the protest of slaveowners who wanted to protect their investment prevented a general slaughter. Twenty-two slaves were hanged together on the same gallows. As they died, some cried out to their fellow slaves to revolt without ceasing until freedom came.

The effects of Vesey's uprising swept the slave world. Laws against education, against assembly, against "benevolence" were passed. Yet sporadic revolts continued to spring up all over the South.

In the North, deeds of Negro courage were stirring hesitant men. Wherever the slave catchers gathered, the free Negroes gathered as well. They were there to offer both moral and physical resistance to the slave catchers; and the silent gathering of black men and women had an alarming and wonderful effect. They fought the slave catchers. They snatched away fugitives. They seemed afraid of nothing, although their black skins exposed them to the violence of Negro-hating men.

Among the free Negroes were men of stature. John Russwurm, the first Negro to receive a degree from an American college, and Samuel Cornish, a Negro clergyman, began in New York in 1827 to edit and publish *Freedom's Journal*. It was the first Negro newspaper in the United States. It was dedicated to freedom and to citizenship for the Negro. Its appearance in the year in which New York slaves were finally emancipated was an event of great importance in the antislavery fight. It went further than Lundy's *Genius* and it anticipated Garrison's *Liberator*. Its editorials gave a pivot to the young Negro leaders who were bringing a firmness and a point of view to this slippery decade. Its office provided a physical sanctuary for fugitives coming up the eastern seaboard.

We Americans have always had a conscience, and now the weak but persistent poundings against this conscience alarmed some and strengthened others. Henry Clay, Secretary of State, was alarmed; for too many hands were reaching out for the fugitive—anonymous hands, women's, men's, black and white—and too many hands were receiving him across those Great Lakes that were supposed to lie so protectingly between the United States and Canada.

Clay protested to the Canadian government in 1826. The Canadian answer was unsatisfactory. The next year Mr. Clay made another appeal. For five months he waited, and then Canada replied, "It is utterly impossible to agree to a stipulation for the surrender of fugitive slaves."

Eight months later the British authority repeated these words.

The third time, the slaveowners in Congress attempted to get some reassurance, and a third time they were refused. They must have felt that many things were conspiring against them, for hard on the heels of this third refusal came *Walker's Appeal.*

David Walker was a free Northern Negro. His *Appeal* was published in Boston. It was addressed to all slaves. In plain language, he urged them to rise against their masters. He urged bloodshed as the only means of toppling slavery.

The effect was electric. To the slaveowner, the *Appeal* was a bare sword. To the antislavery man, it was an embarrassment and yet he knew that it was the inevitable effect of the violence of slavery.

It appeared briefly in the remotest sections of the South. It was discussed in Southern legislatures as though men believed something could really be done to stem the desire for freedom.

North and South Carolina, Georgia, Virginia, and Louisiana passed laws against its circulation. Georgia, in addition, passed a law preventing free colored people from coming into the state and in one day rushed through a law making education for both free and enslaved Negroes illegal. In addition, Georgia offered a reward of ten thousand dollars for Walker, taken alive, and one thousand dollars if taken dead.

On the surface, it seemed as though Walker had accomplished nothing but more hardship for the Negro. But repression succeeds only for a time, and the *Appeal* added to the restlessness which was the worst enemy of slave masters.

These were still cautious days. No one quite knew how to end slavery. Few were willing to come to grips with the law. Many still hoped that caution and persuasion would make slaveowners give up their slaves.

But a changing world was all about them. Violence became the order of the day. Little Lundy was set upon in the streets of Baltimore, beaten, and left for dead. To many people, this became a symbol. Until the brave, peace-loving Lundy was reproduced a thousand thousand times, violence would continue to be the order of the day.

Greater even than the moral horror against slavery was a new factor entering the picture. In the industrialized North factories were being built, textile mills were dominating the economy of New England, and immigrants were beginning to pour in from Europe—cheap, *free* labor.

The Northern free Negroes and fugitives were forced

to work for any hire and they drove down the scale of wages until they were hated by many white working men. Slave agents found unexpected allies among those who wanted no more Negroes to take jobs from white men in the North.

The threads of economics and idealism became so tangled that the friends of freedom realized new thinking was needed, and careful plans. A new era was dawning.

The era of William Lloyd Garrison.

5

GARRISON came from Massachusetts. He believed in right and wrong, and he had no doubts about which was which. He was an uncompromising young man who belonged to the new era of change and reform.

He had listened to Lundy and he had been convinced. His hatred of slavery had come swiftly and finally. He had stood up in a Boston church and said, "I am ashamed of our country. I am sick of our unmeaning declarations in praise of freedom and equality. I could not, for my right hand, stand up before a European assembly and exult that I am an American."

In Baltimore he joined Lundy. There, for the first time, he saw the slave trade in action. He saw New England ships starting off for the South, loaded with slaves; and he saw a native of his own Massachusetts town commanding such a ship. He denounced the ship's captain and was put in jail for libel.

Released, he returned to Boston and, in a small room, put up a printing press, a chair, and a table. He set his editorial in type without bothering to write it out first. On January 1, 1831, the first issue of *The Liberator* appeared, and across the front page lay this challenge:

> I will be as harsh as truth and as uncompromising as justice. On this subject I do not want to think or write with moderation. No! No! Tell a man whose house is on fire to give a moderate alarm. Tell him to moderately rescue his wife from the hands of the attacker. Tell the mother to gradually extricate her babe from the fire into which it has fallen. But urge me not to use moderation in a cause like the present. I am in earnest. I will not equivocate, I will not excuse, I will not retreat a single inch—and I WILL BE HEARD!

Garrison brought out the first issue of *The Liberator* without a cent of capital or a single subscriber. When Garrison and his partner, Isaac Knapp, added up the results of that first issue, they found that their assets had increased by twenty-five subscribers, mostly colored people, and a gift of fifty dollars from a Negro friend.

The greatest asset, however, was not taken into account —that Garrison, as an editor, was a genius. He wrote editorials that set the imagination and the conscience aflame. Men began to climb the three flights to his printing office which was also his home. All kinds of men came: young men, middle-aged men, clergymen, poets—John Greenleaf Whittier was one—and two or three ladies.

Garrison knew that the South, without factories or industry, had to buy everything from the North—from its cotton goods to its slave whips—and he knew that the North had no desire to upset this balance of trade. In every issue he stressed this. In each issue, he struck out against slavery's friends in the North and against the iniquities of slavery. In every issue of *The Liberator*, Garrison reprinted, without comment, news items from the Southern papers relating to slavery; and nothing he could have composed would have struck at the heart as did these candid disclosures, frequently in the form of advertisements. "The subscriber's servant has run away. He had one ear chopped off and his back was badly cut up. $100 reward." Or "$50 reward. Ran away from the subscriber, his negro man, Paul. I understand Gen. R. Y. Hayne has purchased his wife and children and has them on his estate where, no doubt, the fellow is frequently lurking." Or "The undersigned, having bought the entire pack of negro dogs, now proposes to catch runaway negroes. His charge will be $3 per day for hunting and $15 for catching a runaway."

Someone defined the spirit of those years in these words:

"Each age teaches its own lesson. The lesson of this age is that of sympathy for the sufferer, and of devotion to the progress of the whole world."

Garrison spoke for this age. He gave voice to thousands of plain men and women who loved good and hated evil.

In the churches, and at public meetings, they spoke with his voice. They read *The Liberator* defiantly. And back of these white abolitionists stood the Negroes who held up the right arm of Garrison. They nourished *The Liberator's* half-starved coffers. They paid Garrison's debts on more than one occasion. They were friends who gave to each other.

In July, 1831, a National Convention of Colored People was called in Philadelphia by free Negroes and former slaves. They discussed the effects of slavery on the mental condition of the fugitives, they discussed schools and the colonies springing up in Canada and the best ways of extending the work of the underground lines.

Garrison was asked to speak, and he said with his passionate sincerity, "I never rise to address a colored audience without feeling ashamed of my own color. To make atonement in part, I am ready on all days, on all convenient occasions, in all suitable places, before any sect or party, at whatever perils to my person, character, or interest, to plead the cause of my colored countrymen in particular and of human rights in general."

Here his moral power lay—*human rights in general.* The rights of the poor, the rights of women, of children, to be safe; of the sick and the aged to be protected; of thought and inquiry to be unfettered—all these things Garrison demanded in the name of freedom.

The world was stirring with freedom. Ten years before, Simon Bolivar had proclaimed emancipation in Ecuador, Venezuela, Colombia, and Panama, and had watched it spread throughout all of South America, except Brazil.

Britain and her colonies were restless with slaves and would, in two years, proclaim the Negroes' freedom.

A love of political freedom would flame up in Germany, in Hungary, in Russia, in France before this generation was much older. Men would all be looking for a democratic way to live. "The age of sympathy" could not wait for the conservative, the mercantile, the orthodox to catch up with it.

Garrison's vivid challenge came at a time of economic trouble in the South. "Poverty," said John Randolph of Virginia, "is stalking through the land." The value of cotton and of slaves had fallen, and hardship was felt everywhere. Virginia was stirring with rumors of slave conspiracies. In the spring of 1831, she asked for additional federal troops. It was as though she knew that the Black Prophet would strike.

The Black Prophet—whose name was Nat and who belonged to a Mr. Turner—succeeded where Vesey had failed, for his plans were not betrayed.

The Black Prophet had educated himself and he read *The Liberator*.

As a child, Nat had believed that his destiny lay apart from other men. He fasted, he prayed, he preached. He heard voices when he plowed the fields, and his voices all told him one thing: *freedom*. Freedom! he told the other slaves, and he described things he had seen: black and white angels fighting even in heaven.

He was convinced that he had received a portent in August, 1831. He gathered his friends and told them that blood must be shed. For the next twenty-four hours they killed every white person they found, with the exception of a nonslaveholding family whom they pointedly spared. At every plantation they took recruits. Their vengeance was swift and terrible, and the countryside lay paralyzed. For thirty-six hours they were unopposed, and then a patrol caught up with them. Since their weapons were inadequate, they scattered to hide.

Nat lay in the woods for two days, believing that he would be able to regather his forces. When he realized the futility of this, he retreated deeper into the woods where he hid for six weeks.

In the world outside was a wave of savage punishment. "Volunteers rode through the plantations," according to a local newspaper, "running down Negroes, while the more temperate elements in the community protested against an indiscrminate slaughter."

It was horror meeting horror. It shocked everyone who had compassion for black or white. The number of slaves who had a formal trial was fifty-five. Still Nat Turner was uncaptured. Fear lay over the countryside.

Negro homes as far as Baltimore were searched for arms. Raleigh and Fayetteville, North Carolina, were put under military guard. Mississippi, Alabama, Tennessee, Kentucky, Louisiana were filled with rumors of conspiracies. Nat was supposed to have been seen here, there, everywhere. A thousand men were under arms in Southampton County, Virginia, where the uprising had taken place. Two army regiments and units of artillery and cavalry and a detachment of sailors patrolled the county.

All this time Nat lay in a cave from which he could see

mounted men patrolling the roads. One day the dog of two slaves sniffed him out, and within a few hours the news was crackling through the air. When posses came to the cave it was empty, and for ten more days Nat eluded them until hunger drove him into the open.

The trial was quick and as legal as the hysteria permitted. He was put to death. His body was given over to the doctors for dissection. His skin was boiled down for grease.

Turner's revolt was a climax of fear. When people are afraid, as were men who owned slaves, they tend to behave in a way that merely stirs revolt at a deeper level.

Since Nat Turner was self-educated, they decreed that laws must be passed making it illegal for Negroes to read or write. Since Nat Turner was a preacher, no Negro should henceforth be allowed to preach. Since Nat Turner met no opposition along the road, armed patrols must stalk the roads day and night and enter slave cabins whenever they chose.

But, oddly enough, an uprising of Negroes was reported in Louisiana, and two companies of infantry were sent to New Orleans. Had the slaves not heard that discontent was illegal? Apparently the word had not spread to the Carolinas, Maryland, Kentucky, or Tennessee either, nor to Florida, Texas, Arkansas where further uprisings took place.

The nerves of slaveowners were close to the surface. Many property owners left Virginia forever and moved farther South.

Newspapers all over the country cried out against the

bloody actions of Nat Turner. Only Garrison pointed out that it was slavery which had bred this violence. He made it clear that he disapproved of Nat's violent acts, but immediate emancipation was the only solution if the South was not to live in fear of insurrection.

The effect of this revolt never passed away. It reverberated in the memory until the Civil War.

When poor whites now complained of the crops or the poor soil or the competition of slave labor, such complaints were classed as dangerous and subversive. Some were charged with telling slaves they had a right to be free. The first time this was proved against a white man he was to be given thirty-nine lashes; the second time he was to be put to death.

So terrible was this law that it was not often applied in the second instance, but it stood there on the statute books, and white Southern men *were* hanged with rebellious slaves.

Because free Negroes had a certain freedom of movement, they were now forbidden to remain in Virginia and Georgia, even though many had slave wives, husbands, or children. If they continued to remain, they were to be sold into slavery.

All this Garrison blazoned to the world.

The Negro replied to these restrictions as best he could. Schools became secret. Fredrika Bremer, the famous Swedish writer, heard of secret schools when visiting in Charleston. After much difficulty she located one, a dark, wretched hole with a half dozen Negro children. And much later the Union Army, when marching through

41

Georgia, discovered that a colored woman named Deveaux had maintained a school in Savannah for thirty years.

Some slaves still learned through indulgent masters. But masters who permitted this were roundly attacked in newspaper articles and speeches by other slaveowners, for an ignorant slave was the only safe and contented slave. As time went on, educated slaves brought lower prices.

Yet the desire for light is so strong in human beings that it was estimated one out of every fifty slaves acquired some learning. Many learned by crouching down under a schoolroom window and listening to the instruction. Some borrowed copybooks and imitated the childish writing. Some taught themselves from newspapers picked up in the street.

As for the laws against meeting together, these too could be circumvented. There were always swamps or cleared places in the woods where slaves, willing to risk the danger, could exchange information. In every city of any size in Virginia, an organization was formed for the purpose, it was said, of aiding the sick free Negro and burying the dead. By law, Negroes could meet together only by twos or threes. They met faithfully, for it took only one or two to pass on information and advise runaways.

The passing on of fugitives in the dead of the night or the middle of the day still had no name. When the naming finally came, the news spread gleefully. A slaveholder had, in furious indignation, called it the Underground Road.

According to those best informed, this event took place around 1831. A fugitive named Tice Davids crossed the river at Ripley, Ohio, under the expert guidance of those river operators who worked within sight of slavery. He was escaping from his Kentucky master who followed so close on his heels that Tice Davids had no alternative when he reached the river but to swim.

His master spent a little time searching for a boat, but he never lost sight of his slave bobbing about on the water. He kept him in sight all the way across the river and soon his boat was closing the distance between them. He saw Tice wade ashore, and then—he never saw him again.

He searched everywhere, he asked everyone, he combed the slavery-hating town of Ripley where John Rankin and his seven sons kept a powerful watch over the river. Baffled and unbelieving, he returned to Kentucky and, with wide eyes and shakings of the head, he gave the only explanation possible for a sane man. "He must have gone on an underground road!"

The phrase spread like wind along the slave grapevine. Friends of the fugitive completed the name in honor of the steam trains that were then marvels in the country.

Underground Railroad! Why, the very term was a mystery! How could such things be? Was there really a long tunnel, dug miraculously, into which runaway slaves disappeared? The mystification was enhanced by the good humor of the operators who now called themselves "conductor," "stationmaster," "brakeman," and "fireman," called their homes "depots" and "stations," talked of "catching the next train." The words began to cultivate a sense of awe in the uninitiated.

Westerners (as Ohioans and Indianians were called in those days) were more interested in action than talk. The Underground Railroad had now more branch lines in those two states than in any other. The "conductors" learned plenty of ways to harry the slave catcher—as many as the imagination could devise. In Bloomfield, Ohio, a tavern keeper was also a "stationmaster." One Sunday he hid a father, mother, and three children who were at the end of their resources and weak from their flight. He gave them a meal, allowed them to rest, and then put them in charge of a "conductor."

All too soon, the owners of the slaves arrived. Had a fugitive family been seen? They had. Which direction had they taken? The "stationmaster" thought quickly. He said that a tattered family was a bare mile ahead, worn and tired. Their capture would be a simple matter. Why not spend the night and catch them in the morning?

The owner, deceived by the simplicity of this, was only too glad to find a bed. But somehow—who knows how? —everyone overslept in the morning. The landlord had to be roused by his guests and was full of apologies. And breakfast—well, when one makes haste, strange things will happen. At last, breakfast swallowed, the owner, desperately impatient, ordered the landlord to get ready the horses.

The landlord made the long journey out to the barn only to find that he had left the stable door key in the house. It took him ten minutes to find it. When the stable door was at last opened, the horses were found to have each lost a shoe—an amazing coincidence—and the hoof of one was badly broken. The only answer was the blacksmith, but the blacksmith's shop was locked, and no one knew where he was. When, after a long search, he was brought to light, he could find no horseshoes or nails.

By this time, of course, the fugitives were safe.

Garrison became more of a marked man than before. Because he had warned against insurrection, his enemies insisted this meant that he had preached insurrection.

The shock of Turner's uprising—which followed so closely the dramatic challenges of Garrison—put a monstrous spotlight on the abolitionists. The attorney general of North Carolina submitted an indictment against Garrison and Knapp for the circulation of *The Liberator* in that state. It was assumed that the governor of North Carolina would demand their extradition—that is, their legal surrender to him by the governor of Massachusetts. The penalty, it was recalled, was death, for this was not their first offense.

The governor of South Carolina called on the Massachusetts legislature to enact laws suppressing *The Liberator*. The legislature of Georgia offered four thousand dollars for the arrest of Garrison within the borders of the state where he could then be tried under the state's sedition laws. Another reward of fifteen hundred dollars was offered for the arrest of anyone distributing *The Liberator* or Walker's *Appeal* within Georgia.

Garrison called these offers "bribes to kidnappers" and looked to the other newspapers of the country for some condemnation of these actions. He found nothing but silence.

Garrison by no means spoke for all the antislavery men in the country. Many did not agree with his ungloved methods. Many suspected that he challenged even the Union and the Constitution. But others saw in him the only sort of moral challenger who could defeat slavery. Who was right and who was wrong—or who was partially right and partially wrong—will be debated for a long time.

Nat Turner and the Underground Railroad proved, in their different ways, that the unwieldy structure of slavery could be loosened and shaken. Garrison called a National Antislavery Convention to consider all the ways that this fact could be put to the best use.

Less than fifty men met this challenge, and none of them was powerful. They were small tradesmen and teachers, underpaid clergymen, a quarter of them colored men who could scarcely read. But without delay, they organized themselves to help Negro boys to find jobs; they pressed for the admission of colored children into the schools; they attempted to improve and increase the schools already established; they set out to investigate every case of a New Englander who had been kidnaped and returned to slavery and to take every possible step to free him; they appointed agents to sell antislavery tracts.

It took great courage to stand forth in public places as an abolitionist. The abolitionist was the victim of cartoons and personal attacks in an age that knew few libel laws. On the streets he was followed by mockers, and his family had to endure all kinds of insults. His children were shunned in school. At town meetings he was hissed. In churches he was ignored. Everywhere he was treated as a community outlaw.

Yet abolition societies began to spring up all over New England, and agents began to trudge from town to town, and speakers demanded hearings. Many of them were simple men of little education, but they had a burning faith that they were preaching Christian love when they cried out against enslavement.

By the end of that first year, they had survived the stones, the vegetables, the eggs that were thrown at them. Their tracts were being widely read, and men of substance were making friendly gestures. Garrison himself was becoming one of the most powerful men in the United States.

What Luther was to the Protestant church, Garrison was to the cause of freedom. His tongue was as merciless as Luther's and his pen as scorching. He knew only black and white. He grew to be one of the strongest men in America for the simple reason that he touched the mind of every thinking man, whether that man agreed with him or not, and because he translated all issues—political, social, religious, economic—to the cause of abolition.

"Mr. Garrison," a friend once protested, "you are too

excited—you are on fire!" "I have need to be on fire," he replied, "for I have icebergs around me to melt."

Many in the North hated him and all his followers. The South could hardly have expressed more fury. A New York merchant made the reason clear.

We are not such fools [he said] as not to know that slavery is a great evil. But it was consented to by the founders of the Republic. It was provided for in the Constitution. A great portion of the property of the Southerners is invested under its sanction, and the business of the North as well as of the South has become adjusted to it. There are millions upon millions of dollars due from Southerners to the merchants of this city alone, the payment of which would be jeopardized by any rupture between the North and the South. We cannot afford to let you or your associates succeed in your endeavors to overthrow slavery. It is not a matter of principle with us. It is a matter of business necessity. We do not mean to allow you to succeed. We mean to put you Abolitionists down—by fair means if we can, by foul means if we must.

As Garrison said, many years later, it was not the South he fought primarily, but its Northern allies.

6

THE New York merchant who spoke so candidly about money and slaves spoke the truth. The North was keenly sensitive to any change in its relations to the South. Since abolitionists were the enemies of the slaveholder, they were also the enemies of the Northern merchant. This was why mob violence was directed against them.

During the next few years, the Rankins in Ohio would be attacked by mobs over one hundred times. In New York in 1833, when Garrison returned from a trip to England, he had to be taken off the boat secretly, for several thousand New Yorkers were occupied that day in chasing down a small band of abolitionists who were forming a New York Antislavery Society.

Placards had appeared in the city signed *Many Southerners*, calling a counter meeting of the friends of slavery.

The morning papers had been filled with attacks against the abolitionists. A mob formed in the street outside the building where the abolitionists were meeting.

Arthur Tappan, a wealthy merchant but an antislavery man, said that the shouts of the mob could be heard clearly in the meeting room. The delegates were not afraid. The threats merely meant that, when they left, they would have to climb through a back window rather than use the front door.

This handful of New York citizens, undisturbed by threats, passed their resolutions, struck the small match of their hatred of slavery, and looked without despair at its tiny blaze. Later they made their way as calmly into the back alley as though they were going out the front door.

In the summer of 1834, thirty-one houses and two churches in New York were destroyed by proslavery crowds. Placards mysteriously appeared when the mob fever waned, inciting to rasher deeds. A mob broke into the Tappan house on Rose Street and threw the furniture out the window, building a bonfire with the bed linen and the possessions.

In his store Arthur Tappan gave firearms to his clerks, and, as the first stone crashed through the window, they stood at their counters and lifted their guns. The mob fled, but it gutted a church in Spring Street, tearing up pews to use as weapons against the Twenty-Seventh Regiment which clattered through the streets in an effort to bring an end to the riot.

Later that day, they sacked a Negro church and set fire to several more Negro homes. By the end of the fourth day, every regiment in the city was under arms to subdue the rioting.

But the abolitionists were not weakened. The Negroes were not terrorized. The rioters had not cooled their tempers.

The fever spread across the river to New Jersey; up to Norwich, Connecticut, where Negroes were attacked and driven out of town and an abolitionist preacher was drummed from his pulpit and out of the church; down to Philadelphia where the city was paralyzed by three days of riot.

Everyone had explanations for this outburst of violence, and everyone had some truth behind him. Some stressed the fear of white laborers that Negroes would take away their jobs. Some men, of weak antislavery impulses, thought that it was Garrison's intemperate language that fed the flames. Others felt that the time itself must be blamed— "There is abroad in the land a spirit of lawless violence," said William Jay, "which means danger to civil and religious liberties."

There could now be no turning back. In the four years since the founding of *The Liberator,* the abolition movement had become the conscience of the country; and, until slavery was brought to an end, this conscience would not be stilled.

Now a new type of abolitionist was beginning to come forward. William Jay, for example, was the son of the first Chief Justice of the United States. He did not particularly like Garrison, he even thought him a danger, but he believed that the choice lay between Garrison's abolition and the end of constitutional freedom, and he chose Garrison. Edmund Quincy was an aristocratic man of Boston, and he too believed there was no choice. Choosing Garrison meant that he was no longer invited to the homes of his friends, but he made the choice cheerfully. Cassius Clay was said to be the wealthiest young man in Kentucky, yet, when he heard a lecture by Garrison, he turned his back on his political ambitions and stood up against slavery.

The abolitionists concentrated their efforts in pamphlets—some brilliantly written—which were scattered in all directions. They were left by the roadside, in parlors, bars, stagecoaches, railway cars, and boat decks, sent through the mails to all public addresses. Several thousand were posted regularly to governors and legislators, judges, lawyers, clergymen, and editors.

Abolitionists were accused of smuggling handkerchiefs, printed with antislavery designs, into bales of goods addressed to the South, of smuggling pictures, which showed the joys of freedom, to Negroes who could not read.

The slave states tightened all their slave laws and passed new ones. Tennessee now gave ten years at hard labor, and Alabama gave death, for distributing antislavery literature, whether written or engraved on paper, wood, cloth, metal, or stone. South Carolina decreed that no slave who had been north of the Potomac River, in the West Indies, or Mexico, could be brought into the state.

Bit by bit people began to ask, "How much of this reaction is fear of slave uprisings, and how much is it fear that the poor slaveless whites might be persuaded by abolition arguments?"

For, politically and economically, the nonslaveholding whites must be made to feel entirely dependent on the slave power. To cast a great cloak of racial solidarity over *everything* was indispensable to the slave power.

In Charleston, S.C., a mob broke into the postoffice. They snatched a large bundle of antislavery newspapers and burned them in the street. It made a huge bonfire . . . seen all over the country, for it was a violation of one of the most important tenets of the Constitution, freedom of the press, and this shocked many people.

The postmaster was a conscientious man, and he wrote frantically to the Postmaster General in Washington, asking how he could protect the mails. The Postmaster General delayed replying, and when he did, he suggested that the feelings of a community were more important than the mails.

But that was not the oath which the postmaster had taken. He appealed to the postmaster in New York to hold up the antislavery mailings as long as he could to relieve the tension at the southern end.

The postmaster in New York appealed to the Antislavery Society to keep their literature out of the mail. The society answered with the Bill of Rights.

The crisis reached the President, Andrew Jackson. He came out thumpingly for the Bill of Rights but urged that abolitionists be drummed out of society as an army would drum out a soldier who had been stripped of his rank. Newspapers in the South editorialized about that drum court of Jackson's, and Georgia offered twelve thousand dollars to any man who delivered Arthur Tappan across the border. New Orleans raised the bid to twenty thousand dollars. A small ship soon arrived in New York harbor with eighteen Charleston men aboard who talked volubly about collecting the twenty thousand dollars reward.

To many men it was quite natural that the rewards for Tappan exceeded those for Garrison. The Tappan brothers represented the solid, successful, conservative Northern businessman who was, traditionally, the ally of the cotton planter and slave master. If antislavery could influence businessmen like the Tappans, it was a formidable menace.

Tappan showed great courage. His business suffered when other businessmen shunned him. Northern newspapers attacked him. Insurance companies refused to protect his property—and why, indeed, should they, when his stock was so often damaged by riots? So wide was his fame that country people, visiting the city, would enter his store merely to have a look at him.

Every effort was made to halt his activities. A delegation of bankers and insurance men pleaded with him to protect his credit, to protect his creditors, for his business surely could not survive. Everything would be made safe for him if he would merely resign from the New York Antislavery Society. It was said that he thought for a long time, and finally replied, "I will be hanged first."

Violence was certainly the order of the day. In Canaan, New Hampshire, this same year—1835—three hundred citizens whipped a yoke of a hundred oxen and dragged the small Noyes Academy into a swamp. The Noyes Academy had opened its doors to Negro students.

In Boston, one October day of this same year, word got around that a famous British abolitionist, George Thompson, planned to address a meeting of the Boston Female Antislavery Society. The ladies denied it, but placards appeared all over the city calling up a mob.

The women refused to be frightened. Thirty of them, white and colored, met together and Garrison came to address them. The meeting opened with a prayer which could scarcely be heard for the shouting in the street outside. Conservative newspapers later guessed that between two and five thousand people were in that crowd.

The mob broke down the front door and swarmed up the stairs. They cut off Garrison's escape, but he managed to get out a back window. The mob was, on the whole, composed of businessmen (a broadcloth mob, as the newspapers called it); and, to them, some of these antislavery women looked very much like their own wives. The men made way for them, and the ladies departed, two by two, a white woman and a colored, side by side, their hands folded in their cotton gloves, their eyes busily identifying the genteel leaders of the mob.

With the ladies safely out of the way, the mob set after

Garrison. They found him in a nearby carpenter's shop. One man tried to hurl him from a second-story window, but he was rescued by another. The clothes were half torn from his body, a rope was tied around his waist, and he was pulled into the street.

This was a dreadful sight. In Boston, the cradle of liberty, a champion of freedom was marched with a rope around his body. "Don't hurt him!" some cried from the crowd, "he is an American!"

People pouring from the side streets could not see him for the size of the crowd. But those who lined the curb saw him clearly, walking between the two men who held his arms. His face was raised, and a slight smile was on his lips. At the turn of State Street, near the City Hall, the mayor and some constables made a sortie on the mob. The constables dragged Garrison away from his captors and hustled him up the steps of the City Hall.

He sat in the mayor's office until nightfall, looking down on the mob which stirred and shouted in the street below. With nightfall, he was lodged in a nearby jail for protection, and there his friends came to see him, among them Whittier and Mr. and Mrs. Alcott, the parents of Louisa May.

On the wall of his cell he wrote, "William Lloyd Garrison was put into this cell on October 21, 1835, to save him from the violence of a respectable and influential mob who sought to destroy him for preaching the abominable and dangerous doctrine that all men are created equal and that all oppression is odious in the sight of God."

The next day he was released. No such outburst ever happened again in Boston. Too many people had been deeply shocked.

The leaders of the mob printed their justification the next day—"to assure our brethren of the South that we cherish rational and correct notions on the subject of slavery."

At the very hour of the attack on Garrison, another respectable mob was attacking six hundred delegates to an antislavery convention in Utica, New York. But, as in Boston, this merely strengthened the cause of antislavery.

This threat to the very basis of Americanism, the Bill of Rights, troubled many people who had never seen a Negro. For a time, it is true, Garrison had to leave Boston, and *The Liberator* was printed secretly. But powerful men saw in these mobs a danger so great that they could no longer be silent. The Utica mob caused Gerrit Smith to throw in his lot with the abolitionists, and Gerrit Smith was a man of fabulous wealth. Such men were not the fervent idealists that Garrison was. They were hardheaded, practical men who, nevertheless, cherished an ideal of freedom. They now began to think in political terms.

Antislavery societies were forming all over the North. Agents were hired. These agents were zealous men and women who, for their mere living expenses, would go from town to town, lecturing and exhorting, organizing societies. All these societies, born in the storm and grounded in the swell, strengthened the Underground Railroad.

Each member became, willy-nilly, a "station keeper." An abolitionist might be called upon at any time to help a fugitive, although every man who helped a fugitive was not necessarily an abolitionist. That friend might be found suddenly in someone who, a moment before, was the stoutest champion of Southern rights. "I'm a Democrat," one rough-bearded fellow said, coming in a Quaker's store, "but I couldn't stand out against the pleading look in that fellow's eyes."

The full-time friends came by the same humane route. William Cratty, in central Ohio, was deeply moved by a fugitive who had escaped in spite of an iron band around his neck from which prongs curved up and over his head. Cratty began his operations as a station keeper in 1836 and continued them for nineteen years. He claimed to have helped three thousand slaves escape. His reputation spread so far that a reward of three thousand dollars was offered for him if delivered dead or alive below the Southern line. He eluded both the federal law and the lynch law, although he never opened his door until he first knew the business of his visitors.

Many of the points of danger were well marked by now. If the slave catchers knew where to find their fugitives, so did the men of the Underground Railroad. In New York, in 1835, a Vigilance Committee was organized to give its whole time to the protection of runaways. This task fell to a handful of white and colored men. Against a plague of kidnaping, hoodwinking, and terror they calmly arrayed themselves.

The slave trade was flourishing, and slave ships were flying the American flag. The government gave the trade an oblique support by refusing to adhere to the international agreement of right of search. The right of search was directed against piracy, but by it a nation was allowed to challenge a ship believed to be engaged in any illegal trade.

The American government also refused to give enough funds to the Navy to permit an adequate patrol of the African coast, where the slave ships ran things pretty much as they chose.

Many of the slave ships docked in New York. Slave pens were built in private houses where the Africans were held until they could be shipped to the South. The Vigilance Committee knew that the law against the slave trade was being broken, and it set its small strength against this.

The committee sued, and it was thrown out of court. It sued again and met the powerful proslavery forces that dominated the New York courts. The price of slaves was rising. The Vigilance Committee continued its agitation, since New York harbor figured so largely in the slave trade. The committee drew in the best legal talent of the abolition movement. Bands of determined colored citizens snatched fugitives and newly arrived Africans from under the very nose of slave agents. There was no lack of courage. But the abolitionists were obliged to ask themselves whether courage alone was sufficient to set against the new danger being prepared for them: changing laws in the Northern courts.

They had recognized this probable danger after the burning of the mails in Charleston. They knew that they could be so hemmed in by laws that *every* action would become illegal. They saw that all future fights would have to be waged not only for the fugitive but for the protection of constitutional rights, to keep intact free speech, free press, and free assembly. This involved, in most cases, adroit planning, political sagacity, and shades of difference which, to Garrison, suggested compromises.

To him there was only right and wrong. To his zeal and his single purpose, new problems did not exist. Immediate emancipation could not be gained by long-drawn-out legal methods but by moral suasion and the direct actions that went with it.

He was a man of relentless logic, and many of his co-workers felt that relentless logic did not always take into account the perplexities and doubts of the average man who might have only his good will to offer.

The great clanging bell that was Garrison should, they felt, be modulated to the sound of many little bells calling persuasively, convincingly, disarmingly, to the support of the Constitution.

But Garrison moved in a world of pure principle. There were few with the ability to move there with him. He put a strain upon his friends. He threatened to become a burden in a changing world.

The influential new adherents to abolition, and some of the older ones, felt that to make friends was imperative. Appease, they said, as far as honor permits. Do not antagonize. But to Garrison, to see evil meant to strike at it. He saw great evil in the attitude of the churches which opposed abolition, and he struck at them fiercely. This disturbed many of his followers.

Many abolitionists were turning to Congress for assistance. Garrison saw in Congress a stronghold of slavery.

Many abolitionists felt they should work first for the abolition of slavery within the District of Columbia. Garrison would hear of nothing but emancipation *everywhere*.

The politically minded abolitionists were slowly edging ahead of him. They began a heavy bombardment of Congress with petitions—petitions of all kinds relating to the Negro. By 1835, the wisdom of keeping petitions always before Congress and debates continually recurring on the floor was evident. One session of Congress received four hundred thousand signatures to antislavery petitions. This was political dynamite.

Yet there was only one antislavery member in the House, William Slade of Vermont, and in the Senate only one, Thomas Morris of Ohio. On them fell a very heavy burden when the skillful Senator Calhoun of South Carolina arose one day to make a motion to table all these petitions for the abolition of slavery. A similar motion was made in the House.

The fact that four hundred thousand people had signed petitions had taught a hasty and jarring lesson to Northern congressmen. It was obvious they would have to do something to satisfy the growing numbers of their antislavery constituents. The debates in both Senate and House raged for several weeks, and the publicity was "worth a fortune to the cause of abolition."

Many who were not abolitionists felt that, if a choice must be made between appeasing slavery and supporting the constitutional right of petition, the decision must be for the Constitution. And this conviction carried them straight into the ranks of the abolitionists.

When the roll call was taken in the House to vote on the tabling motion, indignant men said they were being required to "vote on a vote to stifle the vote." The motion brought old John Quincy Adams to his feet in shocked protest. He had been President of the United States. To him the abolitionists had been unfailing irritants. But he had not lived his long life to see a gag rule in the Congress of the United States.

He was the only man in Congress who, through his own prestige, could lift the antislavery point of view to the level of patriotism. Freedom of speech and petition was the cry he raised in the House. The end of slavery was the cry he raised in the North. The remainder of his life, he said, would be devoted to this end. "Whether peaceably or by blood, it shall be accomplished. By whatever way, I say let it come."

The motion was defeated.

Within a short time, Personal Liberty Laws were passed in Indiana, Connecticut, New York, and Vermont. They allowed trial by jury to the fugitive, who now had some protection from the sheriff's warrant and the slave catcher's traps.

For the new generation of abolitionists, the Constitution became suddenly the tactical basis of action. The legal minds within the antislavery ranks saw Personal Liberty Laws as the answer to the Fugitive Slave Law of 1793.

7

ELIJAH LOVEJOY is a symbol in American history. He is a symbol of freedom of the press.

In November, 1837, Elijah Lovejoy was killed.

He was a young man from Maine who edited a religious journal, called *The Observer,* in St. Louis, Missouri. A particularly savage lynching of a Negro in St. Louis drove him from a lukewarm attitude toward antislavery to strong and vigorous editorials. A mob attacked his office, his press was destroyed, and he himself was driven into Illinois. At Alton, he resumed printing of *The Observer.*

But southern Illinois was, for all practical purposes, a Southern state. When the newspapers in St. Louis began a steady barrage against Alton, Illinois, threatening to boycott Illinois business if Lovejoy were not silenced, certain Alton businessmen threw Lovejoy's second press into the river.

Lovejoy bought another press. It, too, was thrown into the river. He invested in a fourth, and the waters of the Mississippi closed over it as well.

Meetings were called by citizens of Alton, and Lovejoy asked permission to speak. He spoke very well, but he did not change their minds. His fifth press was delivered at three o'clock in the morning. His enemies blew horns to bring the press-destroyers on the run, but fifty of Lovejoy's friends, who had sworn that this press should not be destroyed, hustled it into a warehouse and barricaded the door.

The following night, thirty of Lovejoy's enemies knocked at the warehouse door and demanded the press. They were told it would not be surrendered. The leader drew a pistol and announced that it would be taken at any cost. Stones were thrown at the door, pistols fired at the windows.

The friends of Lovejoy answered with gunfire. Some of the mob climbed to the roof and set it aflame. Five of Lovejoy's friends appeared at the door, fired at the mob, and scattered them. There was silence. The mob had apparently been awed by this resistance.

Lovejoy and a friend came out cautiously to see if the coast were clear. From behind a pile of lumber a flurry of shots broke the silence. Lovejoy, with five bullets in his body, staggered back into the burning building and died close to the door.

Those shots touched the nerve center of the North. A man defending his property had been shot and killed. The fact that antislavery was involved was incidental.

Death had done what words could not. Abolition was bound now to the cause of a free press.

With this baptism of fire and the first "martyr," an era had closed.

The abolitionists could now tally up a grim success. Two thousand abolition societies with two hundred thousand members were flourishing. The societies did not all follow the same pattern: the pattern was determined by the local needs. But more and more the members were showing a political alertness.

It was abolition votes that decided the election of William Seward as governor of New York in 1838. He was supported, not because he was an abolitionist, but because he had answered certain antislavery questions satisfactorily and showed a tendency to be aware of the straws in the wind.

In the same year, Joshua Giddings was sent to the House of Representatives from the Western Reserve section of Ohio. Joshua Giddings was an out-and-out abolitionist and a conductor on the Underground Railroad.

Giddings was fearless and loud voiced. He pretended not to notice that no committee appointments were given him, that no one asked him out to dinner. He knew what he was doing. He knew how far his constituents would allow him to go. He introduced petition after petition into a restive Congress.

The straws in the wind were so many that Gerrit Smith proposed a drastic step—a new political party, four-square Antislavery.

Many abolitionists protested. They were divided in their opinions. The Garrisonians, for example, asked how any candidate would be able to keep faith with his abolition principles when his first action, if elected, would be an oath to uphold the Constitution—and the Constitution allowed the slave states three-fifths representation in addition to their white franchise.

Three-fifths representation meant that a slave, who had no vote, could be counted as three-fifths of a man when representation in Congress was being computed. For example, this gave ten thousand white men in North Carolina who owned five slaves each, equal weight in the government with forty thousand inhabitants of Massachusetts.

The Garrisonians saw the oath to uphold the Constitution as a dangerous trap. Their opponents in the antislavery ranks retorted that it was Garrison who was putting the simple cause of antislavery into danger by mixing with it many other causes of freedom, and the most troublesome of all the other causes was freedom for women.

The problem of women's rights had irritated antislavery societies ever since Garrison had insisted that the rights of women belonged in any fight for freedom.

We should understand that at this time a woman had few legal rights. She could not own property, she could not vote, she could not legally control her children, she could not get a divorce, she could sign few papers, and in everything she was dependent on father, brother, or husband.

Garrison considered this a form of slavery and insisted that women's rights must be established along with the slaves'. Yet to permit women these basic rights stirred up almost as much fury among Northern men as did emancipation for the slaves among the Southern.

Garrison saw to it, however, that the New England Antislavery Society encouraged women to work side by side with the men. Already there were several women who went from meeting to meeting, speaking from the platforms.

The Grimké sisters had left an aristocratic family in Charleston, South Carolina, to speak out against slavery. Abby Kelly, a fiery little Irish Quaker, Lucretia Mott, Elizabeth Cady Stanton, Susan B. Anthony, and Negro women like Sojourner Truth and Frances Harper were willing to work, able to talk, as clearly aware of the issues as men, and sometimes more skillful in presenting a case. Yet the sight of them on an antislavery platform angered many antislavery men who believed that the women's activities would injure the cause of the slave.

The problem jangled on nerves that were already uneasy. A countrywide financial depression had affected the antislavery societies as much as it had the slaveowners of the South. The New York society was floundering in a sea of unpaid obligations. The Tappans, ruined by the crash, were attempting to rebuild their business. All over the country, antislavery societies were faced with deficits and had no means of paying their agents or carrying on their work.

The more Garrison was opposed, the more determined he became.

Although slavery and abolition had become—thanks to Garrison—the one question upon which every man had an opinion, many abolitionists decided that Garrison himself must be pulled down from his high position. These abolitionists were the new men who saw the future through political eyes and believed that moral arguments must be reinforced at the polls.

This point of view seemed to Garrison a tremendous danger. He opposed it in every way he knew, but finally, at a special meeting of the American Antislavery Society, such a wide split developed that the antislavery ranks fell apart.

With this split, the political antislavery men felt free to form a political party. James Birney, a former slave-owner from Alabama who had left the South and settled in Ohio, accepted the nomination for President.

With the slave power firmly entrenched in the White House, with both Houses of Congress completely dominated by it, the brave new Liberty Party seemed an absurd joke, something too ridiculous even to laugh at. The Garrisonians watched its pitiful showing at the polls with a grim satisfaction. The Liberty Party came up with a bare seventy-one hundred votes. Yet even this small showing indicated that the antislavery movement had come out of its childhood and was preparing to face the problems of manhood. A step had been taken that would lead in a straight line to Abraham Lincoln.

8

WHILE all this was going on, fugitives were not delaying their flight. Among them was Frederick Douglass, who was to become one of the greatest figures in the antislavery fight. The abolitionists did not know of him as yet. But soon they would, to their pleasure and profit.

He had settled in New Bedford, Massachusetts, doing whatever odd jobs he could find. He was young and desperate but determined somehow to turn this cold North into the land of Canaan of which he had dreamed in the South.

As a little boy he had longed for freedom. He had seen relatives beaten, he had watched slaves disappear, he had heard his owner say "it was worth but half a cent to kill a black man and half a cent to bury him."

At length he was hired out by his masters to work in

70

Baltimore. He made his plans. A friend of his, who was a free Negro, agreed to lend him his free papers—the document which a free Negro had to carry with him at all times. This was a tremendous risk for the friend, for a man could be seized and sold into slavery unless he had his papers. But like thousands of Negroes in the South he took the risk to help his friend escape.

Disguised in a sailor's uniform, Frederick went to the station, waited until a train was about to pull out, and jumped aboard. He traveled openly all the way, arriving in New York within twenty four hours of the time he had left slavery.

He did not know which way to turn, but at length he risked everything by telling his troubles to a colored sailor. The sailor took him to the New York Vigilance Committee. He was safely hidden by them until the young woman he wished to marry was able to escape and join him.

The Vigilance Committee decided that the safest place for them was New Bedford where Frederick could follow the only trade he knew, shipbuilding. The friend who gave him a home in New Bedford told Frederick that he must have a last name, and since the friend was reading Sir Walter Scott's *The Lady of the Lake* he suggested "Douglass."

Frederick Douglass was a man of great character and intelligence. He looked like a king. He had a rich, deep voice. He had fire and passion—and he was shocked by the prejudices of the North. When he discovered that

71

even Northern churches segregated the Negro he stood up in an antislavery society meeting and protested with great eloquence.

Garrison was present and heard him and he recognized Douglass' power and grandeur and encouraged him to speak at other meetings. From that time on, the voice of Frederick Douglass became the most eloquent voice raised against slavery. His prestige grew until it became almost the equal of Garrison's.

In the 1840's people were flocking to hear Negro leaders. Most of these leaders came from the ranks of the fugitives, but some were free born.

Ira Aldridge, for example, whose father had been a slave, became a famous actor, although he had to go to Europe to accomplish it. Alexander Crummell had become a student at Cambridge University where he concentrated on classics and theology. James Pennington had studied at the University of Heidelberg in Germany and received an honorary degree. James McCune Smith had graduated from the medical school at Glasgow and returned to New York where he became a physician and lecturer. Samuel Ringgold Ward and Henry Highland Garnet became famous antislavery speakers in all parts of the North. William Wells Brown, who as a slave had been hired by Elijah Lovejoy, became a successful novelist and the best of the Negro historians.

Such men as these were all important in their time. They were all black men who had proved by their lives the absolute justice of equality.

As the 1840's progressed, the value of slaves rose so high that the business of the Underground Railroad fell off. One runaway slave meant the loss of two, three, four thousand dollars. Patrols filled the roads of the South and made escape more difficult than ever. Those slaves who did escape ran through a steel cordon of guns and were pursued as far as Canada.

The railroad was running through greater dangers, too. Fugitives were snatched back under the nose of their rescuers, and their rescuers recovered them at the point of a gun. This border warfare was no less dramatic because its actors were farmers, clergymen, Quakers.

The war was even being carried into the South. Many abolitionists now believed that slavery could be brought to an end only if it were shaken so badly that it collapsed of itself. To accomplish this, they encouraged faltering slaves to escape and then made absolutely sure of their safety.

Calvin Fairbanks was one of the first of the abolitionists to assume the task of going into the South and assisting slaves at the very start of their flight. He became a master in this dangerous business. On one trip into Kentucky he brought out seven children whose mother wished them to be free, and on another occasion he spirited away a girl from an attic room. He provided her with a boy's disguise, put her astride a large log which he had concealed half in and half out of the water, straddled the log himself, and with a piece of board paddled them both to safety.

Fairbanks depended mostly on simple disguises—men in women's clothes and women in men's. He brought out fugitives on foot and on horseback, in buggies, carriages, wagons, "in and under loads of hay, old furniture, boxes and bags." He swam them across the river or waded with them, chin deep.

No fugitive of his was ever captured. When the worst came, it was he himself who was taken, and he served five years in the Kentucky penitentiary.

The Personal Liberty Laws had burst a seam in the Fugitive Slave Law of 1793. These laws, passed in many Northern states, allowed the underground conductors to wage a legal fight up to the Supreme Court. And the Supreme Court, in a tremendously important decision in 1842, decided that state authorities could not be forced to act in fugitive slave cases. It said that only national authorities could carry out national laws. Massachusetts and Vermont promptly passed laws forbidding state officers to enforce the Fugitive Slave Law (a federal law) and refusing the use of state jails for fugitives. Some time later, Pennsylvania and Rhode Island put through the same laws.

Such a victory as this was unusual, for the antislavery lawyers lost on most occasions. But such well-fought and well-publicized cases roused the public and forced people to take a second and a third look at the evils of slavery.

It was plain to every "employee" of the Underground Railroad and to every abolitionist and to every politician touched with the antislavery fever that they were fighting economics. With four million slaves in the country —whose average value was five hundred dollars, but might be two thousand dollars—it was plain that abolition was trying to pull down an investment of astronomical figures.

To set idealism against this enormous economic fact seemed hopeless. But the abolitionists did not give up hope. They simply tried new methods. In 1840, 7,100 people had voted for the Liberty Party. In 1844, 62,000 people voted for the same party.

Things were happening!

In 1836, Texas—which had been settled largely by Southerners—had gained its independence from Mexico, and Sam Houston became its first President.

England and Mexico were quick to offer trade and treaties to the new republic. Neither of these countries held slaves.

But the slave South needed the vast stretches of Texas in which to expand and did not want Texas drawn into the orbit of any antislavery influence. Southerners began to insist, in speeches and writings, that Mexico was planning war, that England was planning economic annexation. Northerners were suddenly roused by the fear that they might lose great undeveloped markets if English trade treaties were accepted.

To these Southerners and these Northerners, annexation to the United States was the only solution. Mexico said quickly that annexation "would be equivalent to a declaration of war," but no one took this threat seriously.

The future of Texas loomed over all other issues during the election year of 1844. The Democrats, who stood a hundred per cent for annexation of the Republic of Texas, won the election. Their victory was interpreted to mean that the people had voted for annexation.

Tyler, in one of his last presidential acts, signed the annexation treaty between the Republic of Texas and the United States. Polk, his successor, a Tennessean, tried to settle differences with Mexico, in order to reconcile her to this move, but his efforts were very half-hearted, and he failed. War with Mexico drew nearer.

The right to extend slavery had won, for all practical purposes. The abolitionists acknowledged this fact with their usual realism. They must now make their opposition to annexation clang like a fire bell in the night.

All through the summer of 1845, the abolitionists held meetings, agitated, kept the question alive, waited for that Mexican declaration of war. Petitions against war were signed by tens of thousands and taken off to Washington.

That winter the Republic of Texas was admitted as a state—"annexed" as Mexico said.

In Congress, Giddings and John Quincy Adams were no longer fighting a solitary battle. Eight antislavery congressmen had joined them. Antislavery was becoming synonymous with free enterprise. Something vigorous was blowing across the eastern hills and the western prairie lands, a new world of factories and railways and sprawling cities.

A generation ago, some nonslaveholding men had nailed two boards together and begun a house and a town out in the West. The town had grown with Northern thrift and industry, whether it was called Springfield, Illinois, or Akron, Ohio, and people had grown with it. These were towns of mud streets and rooting hogs and wandering cows, but they were also towns where people were interested in a larger world.

This was an era of railways—in the North, that is, but not in the South, except for a few isolated lines. Railways brought sewing machines for the women from the new power-driven factories of the East, brought, from Chicago, new harvesting machines which a man named McCormick promised would mean riches for the farmer.

Northern men, sitting on their porches, wanted to know why didn't Southerners have railways? Why didn't they want harvesting machines and sewing machines? Why didn't they get together and make the whole country prosperous? These Southerners—with their three-fifths of a man!—tried to run things in tricky ways, and Northern men said it wasn't fair.

Maybe those fellows in the South had a right to their slaves, but Northerners were beginning not to like the airs they were giving themselves. When a runaway came along, white-eyed with nerves, it was a slap at the high-

and-mightiness of his master if the black fellow were hidden in the corncrib. After all, men of the North didn't need black boys to work for them. They weren't ashamed of their own two hands!

Northerners, sitting around the stove in the grocery store, knew slaveowners were full of tricks. Florida had just come into the Union as a slave state with a constitution that prohibited *forever* the possibility of freedom. Northern men hurriedly presented Iowa, and the balance teetered into place again.

The farmer in Ohio, the artisan in Pennsylvania, the schoolteacher in New England might not have recognized war in the newspaper headlines he read, in the plow he guided, in the spinning loom he manipulated. The shopkeeper in Louisiana, the overseer in Georgia might not have seen war growing with the cotton, moving up the slow rivers and disappearing into northern factories, might not have seen war in the rising price of slaves or the rising value of manufactured goods, but there was something in the air which should have made them alert.

Texas loomed as a tremendous symbol in this struggle of conflicting interests.

For ten years, Texas had kept the country agitated. Now in 1846 a minor incident on the border brought that agitation to a head, and war was declared with Mexico.

Mexico stretched as far north as Oregon, as far east as Colorado. This area, north of the Rio Grande, made up more than half the dominion of Mexico. Now all this territory was being demanded by the United States.

By August, 1846, Polk was asking Congress for more money with which to carry on the war. Certain Northern congressmen seized on this to drive a bargain. David Wilmot of Pennsylvania offered a proviso that slavery should be forever barred from any territory taken in the war.

A roar of protest came up from the South.

That summer Garrison went to England. He sensed that when the showdown came, England must be on the side of the North.

The Wilmot Proviso soon became almost as important as the Mexican War itself. Political meetings sprang up like dandelions. Garrison, back from England, went to the Midwest and talked constantly to Ohio audiences about "No Union with Slaveholders." Crowds pressed eagerly to hear him debate the question with Giddings.

Midwesterners were not afraid of rough-and-tumble political meetings. They knew that the issues of freedom and slavery were becoming gigantic and might cut the country in two. Farther West, in Indiana, the ground had been well covered by antislavery lecturers, telling their stories at meetings in log cabins, in schoolhouses, in places where ox teams were the only transportation, where they had to carry their own supply of candles to light the poor back-country meetinghouses, where roads, made of split logs unsoftened by earth, jogged their wagons to pieces as they looked for a night's hospitality.

As the Mexican War dragged on, it cost more money

and gave people more opportunity to study the techniques of the slave power than the war enthusiasts had anticipated. Antislavery feeling had grown into startling dimensions within the Northen sections of the major political parties, the Whigs and the Democrats. Yet the small Liberty Party was at a virtual standstill. Something had to be done to give it life.

Garrison and Wendell Phillips, a brilliant and handsome Bostonian who had become Garrison's closest lieutenant, had long insisted that antislavery alone would never be enough for a political party. Now others were beginning to agree with them. They were insisting that any Liberty Party worth its name had to support free trade, direct taxation, distribution of public lands, disbandment of the Army and Navy, women's suffrage.

Meanwhile further laws to protect the fugitive were being passed in Northern states; and the boycott of slave products was growing in a small but steady way. The leader in this movement was a vigorous Quaker who came to be known as the "President of the Underground Railroad." His name was Levi Coffin. The demand for free-labor cotton goods made by him had spread so far that he was receiving orders from all the free states west of the Alleghenies.

As a former Southerner, Coffin knew that the South was filled with small farmers, nonslaveholders, whose little patches of cotton were in hopeless competition with the great plantations. He knew that contracts could be made with these small farmers; but that was not good enough, since slave labor ginned and baled it.

At last a gin was bought and shipped to a Quaker farmer in Mississippi who agreed that the whole process should be done by himself and his hired help. Coffin agreed to buy all the cotton in reach of this "abolition gin," provided it were shipped to Memphis, the nearest shipping point that used free labor.

The success of the business brought about its failure. Coffin's supply was not equal to the demand. Large investments could have increased the supply, but anti-slavery men were not the ones with money, and wealthy men were not interested in this kind of free-labor produce.

9

LEVI COFFIN had begun his work of "passing on" fugitives when he was a young man in North Carolina. When he moved to Wayne County, Indiana, he learned that the fugitive was receiving only the scantiest help from white men. He went to the Quakers in his own meetinghouse and demanded to know how they could remain so indifferent. They excused themselves. They were afraid of the law. Levi Coffin quoted Scripture at them—"whatsoever ye would that men should do to you, do ye even so to them"—and proceeded to make his own house a secure haven for the runaway.

It was far from an easy life he set for himself. He ran a dry goods store, and many customers refused to trade with him. But as more Quakers from the South began to settle in the neighborhood, Levi Coffin found increased support. He became director of the local bank. Even his bitterest enemies sometimes needed loans or mortgages. He used his power as bank director to strike many a good bargain for a fugitive.

A week seldom passed without "guests" in his house. The Coffin house had become the converging point for several underground lines. Fugitives would be sent in batches to him from "stationmasters" in the South, the East, the West.

It was a Southerner who first called Levi Coffin "the President of the Underground Railroad." Seventeen fugitives, men and women, had escaped in a body from Kentucky. They had lived through perils, had been scattered by gunshot, had come together again, and had finally reached the Coffin house. Seventeen weary and frightened slaves filed into the Coffin kitchen late one night, brought in two wagons by "conductors." Over seventeen thousand dollars worth of human property sat at a long table and ate the meal that Mrs. Coffin had hastily prepared.

Early the next morning, after the wagons had rumbled on with their passengers, a message came to Coffin saying that fifteen Kentuckians had arrived in the neighborhood, hell-bent on their runaway slaves. Coffin sent the messenger as fast as he could ride to intercept the wagons and scatter the fugitives. Then he settled down to observe the activities of the slave catchers.

Chasing will-o'-the-wisps, they at length caught up with the name of Levi Coffin. Their rage at what they learned was monumental and they threatened him so loudly that a friend of Coffin's arrived in the middle of the night with two loaded pistols to take up his post at the door.

The slave catchers hung about the town, refusing to believe that such tangible objects as seventeen slaves could not be found if they looked long enough. After several days they gave up hope and set out for home. As they passed the plain, square home of Levi Coffin, they made a significant gesture and said, "There's an Underground Railroad around here, and Levi Coffin's its president."

This was repeated so often and spread so far that letters came addressed to "Levi Coffin, President of the Underground Railroad, Indiana."

Eventually Coffin left Indiana and moved to Cincinnati, Ohio. Cincinnati was a half Southern city, slave catchers lurked everywhere. Abolitionists were treated like outlaws.

It was only a matter of days before fugitives were again finding their way to the Coffin home.

The traffic in runaways was enormous in this city by the Ohio River. The dangers were equally enormous. But the dangers did not limit the work to men alone.

Laura Havilland was a Quaker woman who operated a station at the end of Coffin's line. One of her fugitives had begged her to rescue his wife, Jane, so Laura Havilland arrived in Cincinnati to ask Coffin's advice. He suggested direct action. He put her on the ferry for

Kentucky and there, with the help of Negroes, Laura Havilland made her way to the plantation where Jane was a slave.

A free woman named Rachel who showed no trace of her Negro blood agreed to pass Mrs. Havilland off as the aunt whom she was expecting from Georgia. Dressed in shabby clothes, with berry pails over their arms, "Aunt Smith" and Rachel walked boldly to the plantation and joined the slaves at their noonday meal.

"Aunt Smith" did not have much to say, as her Yankee twang would have made her a very doubtful Georgian. It was Rachel who asked permission to take Jane berry picking. While their heads were bent over the bushes, Mrs. Havilland gave Jane her husband's message, and attempted to cover up the wild weeping that followed. When Jane had been calmed, Mrs. Havilland told her to be ready when plans for escape had been completed. Before the day was over, Mrs. Havilland was on her way back to her own home.

Within a few weeks she was again in Kentucky, working on the plans that the husband had drawn up. But she found the countryside in an uproar. A group of counterfeiters had been discovered in the neighborhood, and every stranger, even a Quaker, was looked on with suspicion.

Negro friends told her that nothing could be done until the excitement had died down. She dared not linger, but she did not leave Kentucky empty-handed, for she arranged for the immediate escape of a slave woman and her children. This adventure was a blessing to everyone but the Indiana station keeper who sheltered them. The law caught up with him and, through payment of the enormous fine, he lost his farm and land.

The weeks went by, and Jane did not come. At last her husband, worried, decided to return to Kentucky and fetch her himself. The end is a sad one; for, although he managed to get her and a friend out of Kentucky, they were recaptured in Ohio, and Jane died.

There were many such sad endings, along with the good endings, and the abolitionists were afraid that the tragedies would increase. With the end of the Mexican War in 1848, vast new territories, formerly Mexican—California, New Mexico, Arizona, parts of Nevada and Colorado, territory almost as large as the original thirteen states—were surrendered to the United States in exchange for fifteen million dollars. Mexico tried vainly to include in the treaty an agreement to keep this vast land free of slavery, but the proposal was rejected by a Congress controlled by Democrats.

Yet the South had won only a partial victory. Although slavery was not to be excluded, the South had no positive assurance that it would be included. For the North was not as ready to agree to slavery as it had been ten or twenty years before. The debates on the Wilmot Proviso had made a great impression and people remembered the issues involved. Moreover, something of great importance took place just then which the most determined Southern congressmen could not control.

Gold was found in California.

A wilderness of Mexican villages turned suddenly into a settlement of a hundred thousand lovers of free enterprise. Almost overnight California became an organized body of citizens with a legislature.

While the Southern congressmen fought up and down the halls of Congress to make certain that California would not be lost to them, Californians ratified a constitution which forbade slavery, forever, in the territory. Then, constitution in hand, they asked admission as a state.

The slave power was hypersensitive in those days. To lose so large a state as California was an unprecedented challenge to its power. In the East, where opinions forced national policies, the mobs were again incited by placards and street orators and the resulting confusion was used against the antislavery advocates.

Newspaper offices even in Baltimore, Richmond, and Washington were raided. None of the papers was antislavery, but they—in the very heart of the slaveland —had published articles which criticized the economic effects of slavery. The editor of the Richmond paper was killed.

In Wilmington, Delaware, the slave power at last caught up with the miracle-worker, Thomas Garrett.

Thomas Garrett was a benign, shrewd old Quaker with luminous eyes and an unfailing sense of humor. When he was a young man he had followed the kidnapers of a colored woman employed by his Pennsylvania family halfway across the state and rescued her without ado. During that ride, he said later, the horror of slavery had so beat in his brain that he seemed to hear a voice telling him that his life must be spent rescuing the persecuted and enslaved.

For twenty years he had helped fugitives and yet remained just outside the clutches of the slaveowners' law. No evidence could ever be gotten against him, although his house was constantly watched.

When he heard that Maryland had offered ten thousand dollars for his capture, he wrote an open letter saying he was worth twenty thousand dollars and, if Maryland would guarantee that sum, he would come himself and collect it. Threats of murder were so frequent that his Negro friends established a guard in his front yard. His methods were extreme caution, the simplest of disguises, and a faith in what he was doing.

He must have wondered why the law caught up with him at this time—when he was aiding two slave children —for there was no more real evidence against him now than in the past.

The verdict against him demanded every cent of his property in fines for the federal government. He was sixty years old.

When the sale of his property was over, the auctioneer turned to him and said, "Thomas, I hope you'll never be caught at this again." Quick as a flash, Garrett replied, "Friend, I haven't a dollar in the world, but if thee knows a fugitive who needs a breakfast, send him to me."

In the next twenty-one years, he made an even greater success in business. His friends had bought his possessions and returned them to him. His credit was so good that he got an immediate loan at the bank. His name penetrated deeper and deeper into the South, for persecution was excellent publicity for the underground road. Life seemed to increase for him, rather than to diminish. He became an abolitionist in the fullest sense—a champion of women's rights, an advocate of temperance, a defender of the Indians, and a friend who tried to improve the working conditions of white laborers.

The year 1848 was "the year of revolutions." Freedom was in the air. In Hungary, Kossuth had raised the cry of independence. In Italy, Garibaldi was catching the imagination of the world. In France, a democratic government had brought an end to the monarchy.

Washington was, one evening, celebrating this beginning of the French republic. It was celebrating with torchlight processions and with a speech by the senator from Mississippi—in which he praised "the end of tyrants and of slavery"—when a boatload of fugitives attempted to escape by way of the Potomac. They were seized and put on trial, seventy-eight black men and two white abolitionists. Their attorneys made an effective but futile contrast between the rejoicings in French liberty and the desperate bid of the seventy-eight for freedom. The seventy-eight were returned to slavery, the two white men put in jail.

In Philadelphia, the Craftses arrived, and their story sent a thrill through all liberty-loving people.

William and Ellen Crafts were Georgia slaves who had decided on a daring means of escape. Ellen's skin was white, William's was dark. Ellen dressed herself as a young planter, with frock coat, stovepipe hat. William became her servant. But Ellen was very pretty and this threatened to betray her sex. So she muffled her face in linen, pretending to have the toothache. She put on green glasses. She wrapped her hand in a sling so that she would not be trapped by her inability to write.

The strain of the trip was immense, for it required them to stop at the best hotels. They managed successfully as far as Baltimore. There, when William went to buy their railway tickets, he found that a slave could not proseed into a free state until a bond had been posted by his master. William had to argue the case there and then, while other ticket buyers pressed with impatience behind him.

"My master is in a very delicate state of health. We are afraid he may not be able to hold out until he reaches Philadelphia where he is going for medical treatment. It is out of the question to post a bond, and he cannot be detained."

He waved his hand toward Ellen who indeed looked close to death, and the ticket seller hastily pushed two tickets toward him.

The Vigilance Committee in Philadelphia never forgot the first few moments of their arrival. First the tall hat was thrown aside, then the green glasses and the muffler. Finally the sling was torn away from Ellen's arm, and she danced about the room.

The Vigilance Committee wished to send on the Craftses immediately, for such fine specimens would bring a swarm of slave catchers. But Ellen's nerves suddenly went to pieces, and for several days she could not move or eat.

When she was well enough to travel, they were sent on to Massachusetts. In Boston, they were greeted as heroes. Their story spread North and South, as well as to England and Europe. Antislavery workers, men and women, came to shake their hands and to say, "These are the kind of people we have been fighting for. This battle is worth the powder!"

IO

IN spite of wonderful escapes like the Craftses', in which all abolitionists rejoiced, there was no denying that the antislavery cause was badly divided. And, divided, it could not be as strong as it should be.

Yet the reasons for these divisions was a part of the terrible confusion of these times.

This confusion had been expressed a thousand times and could always be stated very simply: How could a handful of men and women put an end to slavery?

The abolitionists and the slaveowners had always agreed on one thing: that to bring down slavery would be the equivalent of a revolution. Whether it would be a mild or a violent one depended on the point of view. "Disunion!" was the cry raised by slaveowners—and by Garrisonians. "Start afresh" was the milder cry raised by the Liberty Party.

Both agreed that the Constitution was the heart of the matter. Either the Constitution fully protected slavery, as the slaveowners maintained—and as Garrison maintained (calling it a "covenant with death and an agreement with hell")—or it was—as the Liberty Party argued—really an antislavery document polluted by the proslavery forces which controlled every branch of the government.

The angry quarrels between the antipolitical and the political abolitionists made an unhappy sound in friendly ears. To Garrison, political action simply meant compromise after compromise, which would weaken their moral position intolerably. To the Liberty Party men, political action meant steady voting for every antislavery candidate, however lukewarm, and then tireless demands upon him until the government was in the hands of those who would interpret the Constitution correctly.

There was little doubt which side would win. The balances were slowly settling in favor of a new political party, and this meant that Garrison's influence was waning.

The two major political parties were in trouble—mild trouble but not to be ignored. The Whigs were divided into "conscience" and "cotton" Whigs—in other words, Whigs with antislavery and with proslavery sympathies. This split took place because the Southern Whigs had skillfully maneuvered a Lousiana plantation owner, a Mexican War hero, Zachary Taylor, into the presidential nomination and had given the Northern

Whigs no assurance that the spread of slavery would be controlled.

Even the Democrats had their Northern rebels, the "barnburners," who, though no abolitionists, did support the Wilmot Proviso to outlaw slavery in land acquired in war. They acquired their name from the fable of the man who burned down his barn to get rid of the rats, and it was given to them derisively. Their revolt within the Democratic Party was a fierce one, and the "barnburners" called their own convention.

The conscience Whigs joined the barnburner Democrats in this convention, as did a few Liberty Party men. It was a lively convention. It took its stand on a Constitution which was interpreted as an antislavery document. Delegates shouted their slogans "Free Soil, Free Speech, Free Labor, and Free Men." Then they confused many people by nominating Martin Van Buren for President.

Van Buren, when President in 1837, had been a faithful servant of the slave power and was then known as a "doughface"—that is, a Northern man with Southern sympathies. What was he now? Had he changed?

There was little doubt that this new Free Soil Party was a child of the abolitionists. Abolitionists poured money and enthusiasm into it. Even Garrison said, "It is a cheering sign of the times, and an unmistakable proof of the progress we have made under God in changing public sentiments." Yet he was fearful of Van Buren and as fearful as ever of the compromises that politics would demand.

Van Buren carried no state in the Union, and the Free Soil Party sent only five men to Congress. But the fact that a Whig, Zachary Taylor, won the presidency (even though he was a Southerner) and that the powerful Democratic machine had been badly damaged gave hope to a great many.

In Ohio, Free Soil accomplished its greatest truimph by repealing the Black Laws, which discriminated in all ways against Negroes. Now Negroes in Ohio no longer needed to give bonds before making their homes in the state, their children were no longer excluded from the schools; in court they might testify against a white man.

Ohio also sent Salmon P. Chase to the Senate. He was called "the attorney general for the fugitive" because of the many court cases he had fought for the Underground Railroad. In Washington, he met William Seward, elected on a freedom platform from New York. These two men would sit in the cabinet of Abraham Lincoln.

The slave power was seldom guilty of any self-deception. It knew that things were not going well for it. It reacted in its old way: old laws against free Negroes and slaves were strengthened, new laws passed. Newspapers and sermons began to use powerful arguments about the "positive good" of slavery.

These arguments took a disturbing form. They made a semireligious appeal. This troubled white men in the western parts of Virginia and North Carolina, the eastern parts of Tennessee and Kentucky—mountain sections where slavery had never had a strong hold. The men from these sections had been willing to go along with the old notion that slavery was a necessary evil, but they could not accept this new doctrine, that slavery came straight from God.

The slave power needed absolute loyalty. The questions of these mountain men were disturbing. The slave power was also uneasy with President Taylor. A plantation owner with a son-in-law as brilliant and devoted to the South as Jefferson Davis would have seemed a sound bet. But was he? Could he be trusted? He showed inclinations to listen to antislavery as well as proslavery men.

When Congress adjourned in 1849, nothing had been settled. California still stood on the doorstep, waiting to be admitted as a free state. Armed settlers started out from the Southern states, determined to seize California before she could be admitted to the Union with her antislavery constitution.

Many people looked for civil war before the year was out.

Fugitives continued the thin but steady trickle north. In 1849, Maryland, Virginia, Kentucky, Missouri bombarded their congressmen for a law that would close the loopholes.

The abolitionists laughed at this. What kind of law could you make that would keep a Henry Box Brown in slavery?

Henry Brown was a Virginia slave who found all the usual avenues of escape cut off. He hit upon a scheme which could mean life or death. He made a box according to specifications which would allow him a degree of comfort and leave room for a container of water and a little food. A white cobbler, named Smith, who had for several years been aiding fugitives, nailed him into the box and saw him safely consigned to the Adams Express Company as freight to Philadelphia.

Word came mysteriously to the Philadelphia Vigilance Committee, hinting that a box would be on the three o'clock morning train from the South and to look carefully to its contents.

The members of the committee agreed that the strain of the next few hours was hard to bear. When the box was carried in, in the cold dawn, they looked at this uncanny object with fearful silence. What would be inside? Would it be alive or dead?

When the door was locked, one of the Vigilance Committee rapped quickly on the lid of the box and called out, "All right?"

"All right, sir," came the muffled reply.

The witnesses never forgot the next few moments. With saw and hatchet they cut the hickory hoops that bound the box and pried out the nails. Brown sat up quickly but shakily, and no one could say a word. Then, with all the poise of a Stanley greeting a Livingstone in the jungle, he put out his hand. "How do you do, gentlemen."

The story of Brown's escape spread North and South. In Boston, where he was promptly sent, he was greeted as the Craftses had been—a hero. In Richmond, where his friend Smith plied his inconspicuous trade, the news was received with such unbelief that Smith was able to repeat the exploit with two other slaves. But the last effort had unfortunate results. Smith was betrayed and sent to the state penitentiary for eight years.

When Congress met again in December, 1849, only the most unrealistic believed that a clash could be avoided. Every ear, from California to Maine, strained to hear the furious debates that battered against the walls of Congress.

Could the Whigs be trusted? Southern congressmen talked recklessly of seizing Cuba, which lay so temptingly to the south, and making it a slave state. Robert Toombs, senator from Georgia, cried, "We have the right to call on all Americans to give their blood to maintain the slaves of the South in bondage. Deceive not yourselves . . . this is a proslavery government. Slavery is stamped on its heart!"

The small men of the North looked at each other, sitting in their shops, leaning over their plows. The Whigs of the North looked at each other in their law offices and their dry goods stores. The Democrats of the North looked at each other in their factories and shipping offices. *This was madness . . . Cuba . . . blood to maintain slavery!*

The new congressman from Pennsylvania, Thaddeus Stevens, also spoke with a fierce directness: "During the present session we have been told amid raving excitement that if we dared to legislate a certain way, the South would teach the North a lesson . . . Are the representatives of free men to be thus treated? You have too often intimidated Congress. You have more than once frightened the tame North from its propriety and found doughfaces enough to be your tools. But those days are over!"

He spoke in a high, crisp voice, never glancing at the ring of Southern congressmen who had formed around his desk, threatening him not only with heckling but with guns. Congress was often a violent place in those days.

Matters came swiftly to a head. A Virginian offered an amendment to the Fugitive Slave Law of 1793. He said that Virginia alone lost over one hundred thousand dollars worth of slaves a year. He said that in the North were fifteen million dollars worth of fugitives. He wished to put teeth into the Fugitive Slave Law.

It became a long and bitter debate but in the end a great many men solemnly agreed that a fifteen million dollar loss of property was a very serious situation for property owners, even if they were Southerners. And other men felt that if this loss of property threatened the Union something must be done about it.

These two points of view formed a majority, and an immediate effort was made to find compromise solutions which would satisfy that majority. They set to work.

The effect of this produced familiar results. Abolitionists became quarries; mobs started to roam again.

An antislavery meeting in New York was broken up violently. Halls were refused for other meetings. John Greenleaf Whittier wrote to a friend: "The great battle for free speech and free assembling is to be fought over. The signal has been given in Washington and commercial cupidity at the North is once more marshalling its mobs against us."

Ominous political moves had been taking place which indicated that a climax was rapidly approaching. President Taylor died suddenly, and Millard Fillmore became President.

Fillmore came from New York State, but he was a man of narrow ideas and proslavery sympathies. He took the great Daniel Webster with him into his Cabinet, and Webster, one of the Northern giants in the Senate, took care to attack the abolitionists in one of his last Senate speeches.

All the machinery of the government was being prepared for some dramatic move. To the abolitionists it became plain that a program of compromise and appeasement was to be given the country. What could they do?

The country had not been so prosperous for a generation. Businessmen made no effort to hide the fact that compromise of *any* kind had their blessing. Procompromise meetings were arranged in all the big cities of the North.

Antislavery congressmen recognized the size of the fight. They had seen government patronage used for proslavery purposes, they had seen the press whipped into proslavery line. They had heard a round of pro-slavery speeches in the fashionable churches of the North, and they had listened to the endless speeches of slavery congressmen, saying that the slave power would *not* be satisfied with compromise—they wanted all or nothing!

By the end of the summer, the compromises were fully agreed upon and were rolled up into a vast Omnibus Bill. The new western lands would be organized with no protection against slavery, yet with no guarantee for its extension. California would be admitted with her free constitution. Abolitionists held their breaths. . . .

. . . A new Fugitive Slave Law would be passed.

The Omnibus Bill was passed. The Fugitive Slave Law was to be voted on separately.

The fight against it was carried on even through the final voting. It passed the Senate. Still the fight went on. There was a chance it might fail in the House, for it had less than a two-thirds majority, but the floor leaders maneuvered so skillfully that a favorable vote was edged through.

It was a monstrous law. The runaway could now be identified merely on the affidavit of the slave catcher with no effort to prove an identification. The runaway could offer no defense, could not even testify for himself. He was not allowed a trial by jury. The fee of the commissioner who decided the case was to be ten dollars if he returned the slave, and only five dollars if he freed him.

If a federal agent in any way interfered with the capture of the fugitive, he was to be fined a thousand dollars. If the fugitive succeeded in his escape, with or without his help, the federal agent would be held responsible for the entire value of the slave. Bystanders could be forced to lend a hand if a fugitive tried to escape. And friends in the underground work, or casual humanitarians, were liable to a fine of one thousand dollars or imprisonment for six months if they were convicted of passing on a slave.

Many were deeply shocked. Some claimed that the law was made deliberately cruel so that Northerners would refuse to obey it and in this way give the slave states grounds for secession.

The next ten violent years told the story.

I I

O N black men and women in the North the burden was heaviest. Since no identification need be offered by the slave catcher, free Negroes everywhere were in immediate danger. More than fifty thousand fugitives were living in the North—thirty million dollars worth of living property—and intermarried with them were free Negroes.

Within the space of time it took the telegraph to carry the news of the law, the terror spread. The law would not become operative for eight days, but forty Negroes left Massachusetts for Canada the next day, and the exodus continued until it reached immense proportions.

From Columbia, Pennsylvania, half the Negro population left: five hundred men and women. In the northern part of Pennsylvania, the settlement of Sandy Lake vanished completely. From a small town in New York, eighty-two members of the Negro Methodist church, with their pastor, packed up and disappeared overnight. From Rochester, all but two members of a Baptist church went before dawn.

Negro leaders were urging their people to stand firm. Theodore Parker, a famous white clergyman of Boston, slapped a revolver onto his desk and said that would be his answer to slave catchers.

Nothing had roused the country to such violent partisanship—not even the Mexican War. Antislavery men denounced the law in Congress, antislavery preachers denounced it from their pulpits. Walt Whitman, brought up in the Democratic Party, left it in a rage and wrote his first poem, "Blood Money," in the heat of his anger.

Henry Ward Beecher, the best-known clergyman in the country, rode through a snowy Maine night to his sister, Harriet Beecher Stowe, and they sat together until dawn, wondering how his famous name could best be used to protect the exposed and terrorized Negroes.

Men who had remained silent spoke out now as enraged Christians and considered the best ways to help their black brothers.

Meetings were called all over the North—not abolition meetings but meetings sponsored by Whigs and Democrats as well as Free Soilers. Vigilance Committees were immediately set up to safeguard the Negroes.

In Boston they went to work quickly, and many famous men joined the Boston Vigilance Committee. Appeals were sent out for clothes for the fugitives, for employment—for *defiance*. The clergy of Massachusetts were asked, in the name of Christianity, to raise money as quickly as possible. Other towns along the route to Canada were urged to set up their Vigilance Committees without delay.

These committees spread rapidly as far as Chicago. Lecturers were sent out as fast as they could be mustered, and pamphlets fell from the presses by the thousands. In counties all over Ohio, Indiana, Michigan, Wisconsin, Iowa, resolutions were passed that "disobedience to this enactment is obedience to God."

Proslavery men had never expected this deeply moral and religious uprising. They were aghast, for only popular support could make such a monstrous law workable. And how could popular support be forced?

All the machines that mold public opinion were wheeled into position.

"The Union" was laid down as the basis for supporting the law. This appeal was effective. In New York, a gigantic meeting took place, composed mostly of business and professional men. The mayor presided. The Constitution and the Union were put above all other considerations.

Sincere and troubled men, at this meeting, were caught between fearful decisions. For all we know, many of them may have hated the Fugitive Slave Law as much as did the abolitionists, but the choice they made was for the Union and the law. Merchants who refused to sign their names to the call of the meeting or to the resolutions that came out of the meeting were put on a black list.

Many Southerners loved the Union also. The fire-eating congressmen who supported slavery talked as much about the Union as did the Northern business-men. But they could not help pointing out that, although California must be counted among the free states, the new states of New Mexico, Utah, and Texas would vote with the South.

Clemens of Alabama summed it up simply: "A ma-jority in Congress has yielded more than any majority ever before yielded to a minority."

President Fillmore attempted to have the last word. The compromise measures, he claimed, were a "final adjustment." The Union had been preserved, the Fugi-tive Slave Law was sacred, the Whig Party and he were forever pledged to its rigid enforcement.

The fine phrases and the oratory went on for some time. When they all stopped talking, they discovered that the Underground Railroad had not halted for a moment.

If they had not stopped the underground road, what was the good of the law?

Never had the road had such a boom. The "stock-holders" were triumphant. The service was excellent, the accommodations, though not the best in the world, were adequate for the rush. "Passengers come at all hours of the day and night," a stationkeeper announced, "from Maryland, Virginia, Kentucky, Tennessee, and Louisiana."

The dangers of breaking the law had been pounded out by every politician with Southern sympathies. United States commissioners, who would enforce the law, were signing up. Ten dollars for the return of a Negro was easy money.

Yet fugitives came on foot, in disguise, by rail, by boat, by hired carriage, and never failed to find a friend.

Josiah Henson, himself a famous fugitive, writing from Canada, said, "Some have found their way to England, but the mass are flying to Canada where they feel themselves secure. Already several thousand have gone thither."

William and Ellen Crafts were obvious targets for the slave catcher. To recapture such a famous pair would be a dramatic test of the law.

In Boston, where the Craftses had settled, the word spread like fire that slave agents had arrived from Georgia, prepared to seize the Craftses.

The Vigilance Committee swung into action. Ellis Gray Loring, a wealthy lawyer of Boston, learning that no commissioner was willing to serve the Craftses with a warrant, slapped a warrant on the slave agents. He charged them with slander for saying that William Crafts had stolen the clothes in which he had escaped. He asked ten thousand dollars damages.

This was a fine turnabout, and a good-sized crowd went along to watch developments. Bail was set at ten thousand dollars. And was promptly paid. Slave catchers had friends in Boston, of course.

The Vigilance Committee decided that the Craftses must be hidden in a safe place. Mrs. Hilliard, a friend, was asked to go to the upholstery shop where Ellen worked and bring her away on some excuse. This she did, bundling a badly frightened Ellen into her home.

But William would not allow her to stay with the Hilliards. He said, "Mr. Hilliard is not only our friend but he is a United States commissioner, and should Ellen be found in his house, he must resign his office, as well as incur the penalty of the law. I will not subject a friend to such punishment."

The Vigilance Committee agreed with him. Theodore Parker, the famous clergyman, drove Ellen, in the dark of the early morning, to Mr. Loring's home in Brookline. William returned to his store, where he followed the trade of a cabinetmaker, and put a loaded pistol on the bench beside him.

For a week they lay low, the Vigilance Committee alert. The slave agents still searched for a commissioner. Then another alarm was flashed.

Henry Bowditch, a Vigilance Committee member, hurried as fast as his horse could gallop out to Brookline to warn Loring, but he found that Ellen had been transferred, already, to the greater safety of the Parker home.

Garrison meanwhile hurried to a prominent Negro,

Lewis Hayden, in whose home William had been persuaded to hide himself. He found the house barricaded with double locks on all the doors. Hayden's sons had taken up a vigil within reach of a table where loaded weapons lay. Down in the basement was Lewis Hayden with two kegs of gunpowder, preparing to blow up the house if the marshal broke through the guard upstairs. Every member of this household could be sent back to slavery.

Loring hastily slapped on another warrant, charging the slave agents with conspiracy to abduct a peaceful citizen of Massachusetts. The same mysterious and wealthy source provided an additional ten thousand dollars for the slave agents.

It was now clear that if the Craftses were to be protected, the agents must be driven from the city.

A committee of sixty Vigilance Committee members, headed by Theodore Parker, went down to the hotel where the agents were lodged.

That afternoon, the Georgians took the first train out of Boston.

Perhaps they were glad to go. There had been something profoundly disturbing about a city where crowds had followed them shouting, "Slave hunters! There go the slave hunters!"

Among the abolitionists there was no boisterous rejoicing. They knew the Craftses would not be safe in the United States. All arrangements were made to send them to England.

Before they left, the Reverend Parker married them legally, so that they would not be in trouble with British authorities. The entire Vigilance Committee was present at the wedding to give its blessing.

That night Parker wrote a letter to President Fillmore and told him the Craftses had escaped, and asked him how he intended to enforce his monstrous law.

When the by-elections came that fall, nothing played so large a part as that "monstrous law." But men were afraid for the Union, so compromise won again.

It seemed clearer and clearer that in all the land there was no political leader and no party strong enough to make a full attack upon slavery, for the Liberty Party was broken, its leaders confused, the Free Soil was weak. Many said in despair that antislavery must return to 1831 and learn the way of Garrison all over again.

Old work was taken up where it had been dropped ten years before. In the Midwest enthusiasm was rekindled by thumping good antislavery meetings and old abolition songs.

The leaders of the Democrats and the Whigs insisted that the issue of slavery had been laid to rest with the Omnibus Bill. Their greatest concern now was to wipe away from their parties all Free Soil taint, all remembrance of barnburners or of conscience Whigs.

And yet, in spite of all this, the South was uneasy. Could the North be depended on to make the Fugitive Slave Law a success? They had very good reason to question, for all around them were signs of unrest.

One of the most dangerous signs was the unrest among poor whites. Hundreds of poor Southern families were moving west . . . "where I may have my family in a free state, for people do not like to be made slaves," wrote one man from North Carolina to a local newspaper, canceling his subscription.

In the winter of 1850 and 1851, Southern newspapers reported slave conspiracies in Missouri, Virginia, Georgia, Louisiana, North Carolina. In 1851, unrest flared up in the western part of Virginia, as it would again and again until this section became a new state.

The slaveless small landowners joined with the artisans and mechanics of eastern Virginia, called for a constitutional convention, and won two great points that were bitter losses to the slave power.

At this convention, western Virginia insisted upon a larger representation and got it. And they got, in addition, a vitally important democratic gain—the right of all free men of twenty-one to vote. This meant that neither poll tax nor property ownership could prevent them from speaking their minds. This was a great blow to the slave power, for property qualifications had been a powerful means of holding control.

In North Carolina the same issues were raised, for the same reasons. The eastern plantation representatives managed to block passage of a bill giving the vote to all white males, but only for a few years.

In South Carolina, proslavery men were beaten at the polls all over the state—the first time in fifty years—

and bitter words were flung by "free men of the back country against the barons of the low country."

These were Southern white men fighting for their right to earn a living in the smothering atmosphere of slavery.

Other Southern men were realizing that they had to do more than talk if they wished slavery to end. Lewis Paine of Georgia spent nearly six years in the state penitentiary for helping a black man to escape. Thomas Brown of Kentucky went to prison for three years, in spite of the fact that no one testified against him. And John Fairfield of Virginia wandered through the border states, setting slaves onto the underground road.

Fairfield deserves a book to himself. His relatives were all slaveholders, but when John became a man he decided to live in the North, away from slavery. As a child, his dearest friend had been a slave boy named Bill. They had talked many times of an escape for Bill. So when Fairfield left Virginia, Bill left also. Fairfield went with him as far as Canada, and then returned to Ohio.

A perverse impulse caused Fairfield to return home briefly. He found that his uncle, certain of his guilt where Bill was concerned, had sworn out a warrant for his arrest. He had to get out of the state as fast as possible, and he did so, but he took a batch of slaves with him.

He brought them safely to Canada, and his career began.

Because he was attractive, debonair, obviously a gentleman, he was an immense success at his new profession, for no master saw in him a danger. As a matter of fact, he made these escapes his means of living. He hated slavery, and it seemed proper to make his hatred work for him. Fugitives in Canada brought him their savings in exchange for assurances that relatives would be conducted to freedom. He never failed them.

He used many disguises. He lived for long periods in various neighborhoods, making himself thoroughly familiar with the people and the terrain. He seldom carried off a mere one or two slaves. He preferred whole companies.

He preferred his fugitives to be strong and reckless, willing to fight if necessary. Two Negroes who posed as his personal slaves aided in an elaborate escape of twenty men, during which Fairfield, passing as a salt trader, led the slave catchers in pursuit of the fugitives, being careful to lead them in the direction he chose.

When Fairfield discovered that a number of mulattoes and quadroons, living in scattered sections of Virginia, Maryland, and the District of Columbia, wished to escape, he resolved on a daring move.

He ordered wigs and make-up from Philadelphia, set the Maryland group onto the white cars of a northbound train, after carefully disguising them as white people, took himself to Washington, and prepared the second group in the same way. He then went on to Harpers Ferry, where the third group had managed to assemble.

The first two groups got through safely, but on the third attempt, slave masters got wind of his plot. They made a gesture almost as dramatic as Fairfield's own. They hired an engine and a special car to chase the Pittsburgh express. But Fairfield was, in some fashion, warned. The slave catchers saw the express pull into Pittsburgh; but, before it had fully stopped, Fairfield and his "clients" spilled out of the car and scattered in all directions.

Twice he was betrayed and arrested, twice he escaped from jail. He gathered his fugitives from Louisiana, Alabama, Mississippi, and Georgia, as well as from the border states. His health collapsed, he was wounded many times, yet he refused to give up.

His friends were the colored people. He lived with them and for them. Levi Coffin knew him well and trusted him implicitly. Once Fairfield hid twenty-eight fugitives in the hills around Cincinnati, and Coffin got them safely away by hiring a hearse and buggies and forming a funeral procession. It is believed that Fairfield was killed leading an uprising of slaves in Tennessee just before the Civil War.

By 1851, it was plain that the Fugitive Slave Law was a failure. Not only was the Underground Railroad running at full capacity, but influential men had begun to fight the law on every front.

Richard Henry Dana said good-by to rich legal clients so that he could devote all his skill to the underprivileged. Rutherford B. Hayes, later President, gave richly of his time for any fugitive slave who needed his help. As case after case came up for hearing, celebrated lawyers were on hand to find every loophole of escape, to see that every humane appeal had been made as ringingly as possible.

Wagons were built to conceal fugitives, hidden rooms were constructed in houses, employees on bona fide railways used baggage compartments to hide fugitives and sometimes distributed tickets so that they could travel openly as passengers.

Underground railroad stations were usually indistinguishable from any other house; but, as the tension increased, as the fugitives poured up the lines, reaching their peak in this decade, many ardent abolitionists gave their lives so completely to the work that even their houses acquired a new appearance.

John Morris of Ohio, for instance, dug a tunnel from his home to his barn so that fugitives, surprised at the house, would have a chance to crawl to safety. He built an ingenious network of false walls in his attic. Other conductors built trapdoors into the cellars, or false cupboards over brick ovens, or sliding panels where firewood was ostensibly kept.

All over the North new branch lines were opening up, carefully staffed, leading to the colonies in Canada. The lines honeycombed the North, spelling "danger" and "courage." More and more often a pistol now lay strapped to a conductor's hip, a rifle lay within reach of his hand as he slept at night.

In Boston Thomas Sims, a seventeen-year-old fugitive

from Georgia, was arrested and jailed in the Boston Courthouse with a guard big enough to care for a dozen prisoners.

The sympathy of Boston ran high. The Vigilance Committee attempted a rescue and failed. The law required that Sims be returned to slavery, and he was taken in the dead of night to the ship which waited in the harbor to sail for Savannah.

This recapture stirred emotions at a very deep level. So strong was the feeling for the boy and so strong the resentment against the judge who had sent him back that the shopkeepers in Boston refused his "Judas" money and, for days, the judge and his family could buy nothing in Boston.

At the next senatorial election, Massachusetts did what it could to wipe out the terrible shame of losing Sims.

Daniel Webster, the man who had supported the Fugitive Slave Law, was administered a terrible rebuke; Charles Sumner, the friend of Garrison, a man one hundred per cent for abolition, was elected to Webster's old seat in the Senate.

12

THE day Charles Sumner took his seat in the Senate, men turned frankly to stare at him. He was a symbol of the new times, not only because as an out-and-out antislavery man he had "defeated" the great Daniel Webster, but also because he represented the new power in the North, a rich, aristocratic, influential man who was putting his prestige and his power into the fight against slavery.

The Washington to which he came was a muddy, overgrown village where slavery was dragged as a bargaining agent from senator's office to senator's office, and where the situation was freely and popularly summed up in five words: "In Washington, slavery rules everything."

Sumner had no party, for the coalition of Northern

Democrats, Whigs, and Free Soil Party that had elected him was bound to fall apart before the next election. His enemies believed they had only to wait in order to destroy him easily.

Within five weeks he made his first speech. He demanded the repeal of the Fugitive Slave Law. Within a year, Sumner was the most hated man in Washington (according to his contemporaries) and one of the most powerful, for he was the very incarnation of the antislavery conscience.

This conscience was almost as visible as a man's arms and legs.

It was this conscience which the abolitionists relied upon to change the future. "I believe in the twenty million," Wendell Phillips said, speaking of this conscience and the common man. "They will arrange the question which politicians have sought to keep out of sight. It is a great thing to keep alive a protest. The antislavery cause does not seem to move, but like the shadow on the dial, it gets to twelve o'clock at last."

The shadow was soon to move. A shy, impractical woman wrote a book, and it affected the whole world.

Uncle Tom's Cabin was the story of slavery. Its author, Harriet Beecher Stowe, said that it sprang straight out of life, that the characters were living people.

Mrs. Stowe had lived in Cincinnati, and she had often visited the "Shelby" plantation in Kentucky. She had friends among the slaveowners. She knew that many of them were kind and loved their slaves. But kind masters died, as she said in her novel, or fell into debt, and then the slave moved into darkness and dread.

Second only to the character of Tom was Eliza. In the book she ran away from her owner and, with her child, escaped across the frozen Ohio River in the midst of winter. She was assisted by an Underground Railroad conductor who kept constant watch above the river. Anyone who lived in the Ohio Valley recognized John Rankin in this description, and it was John Rankin himself who had told Mrs. Stowe of the blood-chilling sight he had watched from his hillside—a woman struggling from ice floe to ice floe, sinking sometimes to her waist, dragging herself along, and all the time carrying a child. Simeon Halliday, the Quaker who organized rescues, was identified by every abolitionist in the Midwest as Levi Coffin. Simon Legree, the cruel overseer on the Deep South plantation, was drawn from letters written to Mrs. Stowe by her brother Charles who told her of Mississippi horrors he had witnessed, and of an overseer whose cruelty was notorious.

As for Tom . . . the Tom of Mrs. Stowe's novel was a young man, not the half-comic, white-haired figure that the name has come to suggest. Tom entered her heart the moment she met the great, black, slow-speaking Josiah Henson in Boston, a fugitive who was to become a leader in the antislavery ranks.

Henson told her of his father who, with his ear nailed to a post, had been beaten into unconsciousness, of his mother sold to another master. He confirmed Rankin's story of Eliza and of her husband (who is called George Harris in the book)—he had known them well in Canada. Eliza had died, but her husband, fair as a white man, traveled and lectured with Henson.

Mrs. Stowe knew what she was writing about when she wrote of Tom. Her Tom, like many slaves, was offered the chance to escape but preferred to remain in the South and assist those weaker than himself. Mrs. Stowe's Tom helped two slaves onto the Underground Railroad, others he helped to endure their enslavement. He was a man of courage and power.

Mrs. Stowe understood slavery. She steadily maintained that her story was fictional only in style, not in content.

Eight presses ran night and day to supply the demand for her book. It was translated into twenty-two languages. In Great Britain and her colonies alone, one and a half million copies were sold. In some countries it was considered so dangerous in its ideas that it was banned. But its effect spread around the world, and American slavery was never the same again.

Everything was pouring into the antislavery mill as it never had before. Songs, plays, books told the antislavery story. Women were taking a stronger and stronger part in the whole struggle, and everywhere the ferment of change could be felt.

In this decade—the 1850's—women whose names ring in our history were standing up to their full height.

Susan B. Anthony and Lucy Stone and Elizabeth Cady Stanton were fighting the twin fight for women's suffrage and for Negro emancipation. Dorothea Dix was pleading up and down the country for the care of the insane; Emma Willard was struggling to establish a better education for women, Jane Swisshelm was defying Western mobs in order to gain an equal place for woman journalists, Harriet Tubman was making the magic of her name ring down the invisible rails to freedom.

Harriet Tubman was one of the greatest freedom fighters of them all. A slave woman of Maryland, she escaped, and her own flight set the pattern for her future. It was a long, dangerous future which stretched through the Civil War and included nineteen returns across the border to lead out escaping slaves.

Harriet Tubman had been injured in the head by a drunken white man, and she never knew when she might lose consciousness. Yet the miracle was that she led over three hundred slaves into freedom, and lost not a one. The reward for her capture mounted to forty thousand dollars, but Harriet was never afraid. "Just as long as God wants to use me, He'll take keer of me."

These were heroic women, and they filled the air with their pleas for a new freedom. When all these desires and these hopes of freedom-loving men and women came together, Garrison's work would be done.

Portents were in the air. The first blow of the Civil War was struck in Kansas in 1854.

Between the Missouri River and the Rocky Mountains lay land enough to form six states, land that was Indian territory called Kansas and Nebraska. Men and their possessions—immigrants pouring in from Europe, Yankees pushing out to the frontier, slaveowners struggling to grow cotton in the eroded soil of Georgia and South Carolina—were all hungry for this land.

By the terms of the Missouri Compromise, thirty-odd years before, this land belonged to freedom.

Stephen Douglas was a congressman from Illinois who was exceedingly ambitious. He was also adroit and clever. He urged that the Kansas-Nebraska settlers be left to draw up their own constitution and determine under what system they wished to live. This sounded both democratic and moderate. Men nodded their heads and were taken in.

But suddenly they all sat up with a start. What was Douglas proposing? Was he not *really* proposing civil war within the confines of the Kansas-Nebraska territory? Could any reasonable man believe that a state constitution could possibly represent both freedom and slavery, or that settlers from the slavelands and settlers from the free-soil North would yield their points of view without bloodshed? What about the Missouri Compromise?

The North protested with a shout. The South had, at first, regarded Douglas's proposals as a trick; but, when the indignation of the North rose to such a clamorous height, they realized that the "doughface" Douglas had, by a tricky political maneuver, offered them a rich prize.

For four years the country had believed that peace and unity had been bought in 1850.

For thirty years, the country had also believed that the Missouri Compromise locked slavery out of the North.

Now these two compromises seemed delusions. "Nebraska" became a louder cry than "Texas" had ever been.

The antislavery men were not alone in their fight now. Memorials and protests beat in a torrent against Congress. Party lines were broken. Opponents of the Kansas-Nebraska Bill made strange friendships.

Douglas was astonished, but for him there was no turning back. His own interests and investments—real estate, railroads—had been brought too closely into his plans. Jefferson Davis, the Secretary of War, persuaded the new President, Franklin Pierce, to throw the full weight of the administration behind Douglas' bill. This was an age when politics was at a rough level, and fisticuffs were popular on the floor of Congress.

No one seemed to know what to do. The Missouri Compromise became almost as sacred as the Constitution. If the Missouri Compromise could be thrust aside, then what could control the slave power?

Cries for political action rose higher and higher. In Ripon, Wisconsin, a meeting resolved that if the Kansas-Nebraska Bill were passed, old party organizations must be thrown to the winds and a new party organized on the sole issue of the nonextension of slavery. The name "Republican" was suggested.

Petitions and memorials against the Kansas-Nebraska Bill continued a steady assault on Congress, where Stephen Douglas was jamming his way through to his ambition—the Democratic presidential nomination. At five o'clock one morning, after seventeen hours of continuous debate, the Missouri Compromise was repealed, and the Kansas-Nebraska territory was thrown open for a war between the settlers.

To many Northerners the shock tore at their roots. All the heartbreak, all the drama, all the pleas of antislavery men became, overnight, the rallying point of a million men. The political excitement that was born that day did not reach its climax until six years later when the swirling torchlights of triumphant Republicans proclaimed the election of Abraham Lincoln.

On May 22, "against the strongest popular remonstrances, against an unprecedented demonstration of religious sentiment," the Kansas-Nebraska Bill became law. Two days later, in Boston, the slave power was shown the temper of the North.

13

IT was a quiet, late afternoon, and all over the city people were going home to their dinners. Anthony Burns, a Negro, locked up his employer's shop and started down the street. Five minutes later he was seized by six men and carried struggling a few feet to the courthouse where a marshal, with a drawn sword, motioned them hurriedly up the steps and closed the door.

The Vigilance Committee did not hear of this until the next morning. Then they moved fast. Richard Henry Dana, the attorney for the committee, hurried to the courthouse. Within a matter of minutes, the word spread through the city.

So the slave hounds were at it again! They wanted everything—they wanted Nebraska, they wanted the North, they wanted a poor colored fellow who had managed to escape them!

Before nightfall, Burns's name was on its way across

the country, for his name had, in these few hours, become a symbol for the free North.

The Vigilance Committee attempted to rescue Burns by a raid on the prison. It failed because too many men wished to take part, and confused the plan. The day after it failed, the courthouse square resembled the scene of a battle. A troop of infantry, a company of marines, two companies of artillery surrounded the building. Sentries guarded every entrance to the courthouse and filled the corridors. Two small fieldpieces were planted in the square.

When the trial began, the corridors of the courthouse were so filled with soldiers that the friends of Burns could scarcely move. The trial lasted for three days in an atmosphere of tense nerves and frayed tempers. Rumors filled Boston. More rescue attempts would be made . . . the owner of Burns would be driven out of town . . . abolitionists had been selected for assassination. . . .

Respectable people hissed the soldiers who filled the streets. Negro and white waiters refused to serve food to the troops on guard. Many abolitionists were arrested for disturbing the peace. The crowds were increased by others from nearby towns, all of whom expressed their hatred of the soldiers and of slavery.

The owners of Burns took these things into account and opened negotiations for his sale. But the United States Attorney General intervened. He sent word from Washington that Burns must be convicted and returned to Virginia.

A double guard stood over Burns, for it seemed as though every one in the North was his friend. Dana's defense was eloquent. But three days later the United States commissioner gave his decision: *return to slavery.*

In the courtroom a terrible groan went up. It was echoed by the crowds outside. The authorities took a look at these crowds moving restlessly through the streets and ordered a battalion of light dragoons, twenty-two companies of artillery and infantry, and a corps of cadets to be paraded on Boston Common. Also a detachment of soldiers was sent down State Street to notify every merchant and businessman that he must close his business for the day and leave an empty store. The crowd still gathered. The soldiers had orders to fire if the crowd became unruly.

At eleven o'clock that morning the clearing of the streets began. Eleven rounds of powder had been allotted to each soldier, and he was instructed to load his gun there in the street, before the eyes of the crowd. A cannon was rolled into courthouse square.

It took three hours to clear the streets. Dana was not allowed to approach Burns. But Dana could see the company of marines and the marshal's special posse of "Southern gentlemen" which formed a hollow square. He saw Burns move into this square. Behind him, Dana saw two more platoons of marines, a fieldpiece, and a regiment of artillery.

The soldiers, the horses, the guards, the prisoner moved into State Street, and a long rising moan greeted them. "Shame—shame—shame!" The crowd pressed forward.

The roofs were dark with people. Twice soldiers charged with bayonets. As the soldiers passed, the crowds on the street fell in silently behind them, and fifty thousand people were marching when they reached the waters of the bay.

The government steamer lay at the wharf. As Burns was taken hurriedly aboard and pushed into a cabin out of sight, church bells began to toll, and other bells around the bay picked up the sad good-by.

It cost the government forty thousand dollars to return Burns to slavery. "A few more such victories, and the South is undone," said the Richmond *Enquirer*.

The only bright thing in all this was that Burns was bought by a sympathizer, who brought him out of the state and set him free. He came back to Boston, paid his respects to all his friends, went to Oberlin College in Ohio for an education, and was at last ordained a Baptist preacher and sent to Canada as a missionary among the fugitives.

Wendell Phillips wrote bitterly: "The slave power will have Cuba in a year or two, and Mexico in five. . . . The future seems to unfold a vast slave empire united with Brazil. I hope I may be a false prophet but the sky was never more dark."

What he was saying was that slavery controlled Congress, the Supreme Court, the Army and Navy. By 1860, 11 of our 16 Presidents had been slaveholders, 17 of our 28 judges of the Supreme Court, 14 out of 19 Attorney

Generals, 21 out of 33 Speakers of the House, 80 out of 130 of our ambassadors.

Three hundred fifty thousand slaveowners had made themselves spokesmen for the eleven million inhabitants of the South. Cotton was king, and Ralph Waldo Emerson wondered whether it would be freedom or slavery that would, in the end, be abolished.

Nearly two billion pounds of cotton were produced that year—1854. "The lords of the loom and the lords of the lash," as Sumner called the millowners and the slaveowners, North and South, were making more money than ever before.

Yet that fall of 1854, the Democratic Party was so badly beaten at the polls in the free states that the slave power was alarmed. The word spread swiftly: *take the new territories without delay!*

If free labor won Kansas, the defeat of the slave power would begin.

Missourians poured into the Kansas territory. They staked their claims before the free labor men, hurrying as fast as they could over the trails and down the river, arrived with their plows and seed.

That fall the territory had its first election. Proslavery instructions were clear. The senator from Missouri urged a Missouri crowd to cross into the territory that day and rush the polling places. "Enter every election district of Kansas and vote at the point of the bowie knife and the revolver. The slaveholding interest wills it, from which there is no appeal."

The free labor men were outraged. More immigrants was the only answer. They thought they were prepared when the March elections came around, but they were still inexperienced in frontier violence.

In the second proslavery invasion from Missouri, one thousand men swooped down on Lawrence, Kansas, alone. A Congressional investigating committee later reported that only one-sixth of the votes were valid. The free-state representatives who managed to survive the balloting were promptly unseated by the territorial legislature which, without further delay, adopted the Missouri slave code as the law for Kansas. In addition, Black Laws were put on the statute books, plus a death penalty or ten years' imprisonment for aiding a fugitive, and two years' imprisonment for possessing abolition books, pamphlets, or newspapers.

Free-state men responded promptly. Within the next three years, three hundred fugitives, mostly from Missouri, passed through the dangerous and exposed stations of the Kansas railroad.

Men lived with guns at their sides. Women were trained to shoot. Steady immigration from the North challenged the proslavery domination. Slavery men were sending out calls to the South for reinforcements. "Civil War of the fiercest kind will soon be upon us. . . . We must have the support of the South. . . . We are fighting the battles of the South. . . . Let our young men come on in squads as fast as they can be raised and armed."

Two governments now struggled to control the Kansas territory, for free-state men had drafted their own constitution to fight the Black Laws.

It was becoming increasingly obvious that only violence could hold the territory for slavery. The abolition town of Lawrence was sacked.

Gutted, burning Lawrence sent a wave of anger across the country. Sumner, in the Senate, thundered out his rage, and pounded out names with his fist—Douglas, senator from Illinois, Butler, senator from South Carolina—and called them the real murderers of the men of Lawrence. The fires were still licking about the houses of Lawrence as he flung out his raw, shocking words. Two days later, young Preston Brooks, a representative from South Carolina and a cousin of Senator Butler, found Sumner writing in his seat in the Senate, came behind him, and beat him over the head with a walking stick.

Sumner, lying in the aisle bleeding and unconscious, reduced the whole vast struggle to simple terms: Brooks symbolized slavery; attacks against defenseless men, midnight assassinations, and guerrilla warfare were a challenge to free men everywhere.

Two days after Sumner's beating, John Brown and his sons swooped down on Pottawatomie, Kansas, a proslavery town, and avenged Lawrence and Sumner. It was a bloody and ruthless revenge, a midnight raid, in which five proslavery settlers were dragged from their beds and put to death with an old army cutlass.

John Brown was like a thin, unquenchable flame in his

131

hatred of slavery. To him it was the greatest evil the world had ever known. He had the power to move men deeply because he made freedom a passionate reality and because he was afraid of no one. A free Kansas had become his very life blood. To free Kansas, even with fire and sword, was, for him, to do God's work.

His attack on Pottawatomie meant that war was on with a vengeance. Bands of Missourians threw pickets across the borders of Iowa and Nebraska. They shot at immigrants from the East, they blockaded the Missouri River and sent down it, tied to logs, any who attempted to pass into Kansas.

The political battle in the world outside took fire from the fight in "bleeding Kansas."

When the newly formed Republican Party called its convention in June, 1856, the delegates stressed the horrors of Kansas and demanded a return to the "self-evident truths of the Declaration of Independence." They needed a hero to dramatize their cause, and they nominated John C. Frémont, the explorer, for President.

The Democrats passed up Stephen Douglas, to his bitter chagrin, and selected the aged and complacent James Buchanan.

Few campaigns in American history were as raw as this one. All the bitterness of the past ten years had accumulated to breed excitement and dark forebodings.

To the Republicans, it was a crusade (although they failed to mention the Fugitive Slave Law, and this angered many abolitionists). To the Democrats, it was a supreme challenge to power.

Republicans had the support of liberal Northerners. They attempted to rally the working class as well. The Democrats did what they could to frighten the moneyed interests with threats of chaos and disunion.

The year 1856 was another year of restlessness within the South. A newspaper correspondent claimed that "the slaves are in a state of insurrection all over the country. . . . The ball is moving, and they have heard the sound and intend to keep it moving." From Tennessee, a correspondent wrote, "certain slaves are so imbued with the fable [that Frémont would bring them forcible assistance] that I have seen them smile when being whipped and have heard them say, 'Frémont can hear the blows.' "

But these supporters of Frémont could not vote for him, and the threat of secession won for the country another proslavery President.

Buchanan was a serious blow to those mild-tempered people who had clung to the belief that slavery might be overthrown without fire and sword. Disillusionment ran through the North.

For twenty-five years abolitionists had appealed in every way they knew to break the power of slavery. For two years "bleeding Kansas" had been appealing to the North. For months, Republicans had been spending hundreds of thousands of dollars to expose the stranglehold of the slave power.

But still the people had brought the slavery Democrats back into power. Was there no hope?

14

THE darkness grew deeper when the Supreme Court said that it had made its decision in the Dred Scott case . . . and announced the decision.

The words that Chief Justice Taney read, in his black-robed splendor, with his eight black-robed colleagues stretched out to right and to left of him, could be summarized briefly: "The black man has no rights which the white man is bound to respect," . . . "the rights of the Declaration of Independence do not relate to the Negro, for whom citizenship is impossible," and finally, "Congress has no power to abolish or prevent slavery in any of the territories."

These words were chilling. The question had seemed so simple. Dred Scott, a slave, had been taken by his master into Illinois, in 1834, and into Minnesota in 1836, both free states. When he had been forcibly taken back to the slave state of Missouri in 1838, he claimed his freedom, as he could do under the Northwest Ordinance and the Missouri Compromise. The case had dragged on for years.

The legal decision could have been as simple as the provisions of the Missouri Compromise. But the Compromise had been done to death. Now seven proslavery justices settled not only the slave status of the Negro but the question that had torn Kansas apart.

The two dissenting justices wrote a vigorous rebuke to the decision, recalling that Africans had at one time been voting citizens in nearly every one of the original thirteen states, and they declared the Negroes' rights to be inviolate.

Very few people doubted the political motives that lay behind the decision. The North was deeply disturbed. Newspapers demanded to know if this was also the end of white men's freedom. The courts of Ohio and New York promptly declared that the Negro was free the moment he stepped across the state line.

Frederick Douglass put into words the defiance of abolitionists, white and colored. "This very attempt to blot out the hopes of an enslaved race may be one necessary link in the chain of events leading to the complete overthrow of the whole slave system."

Along the underground line the reaction was immediate, as it always was. When a deputy with nine assistants plunged into Mechanicsburg, Ohio, in pursuit of Addison White, a fugitive, he was met by gunfire from White, concealed in the attic of Udney Hyde's home.

When the deputies retreated before the gunfire, they ran into the arms of the "whole abolition town of Mechanicsburg"—young men with clubs, old men with pitchforks, women with cooking pans. The deputies left hastily. When they returned with reinforcements, they found that Addison White had taken off for Canada and that Hyde was safely hidden by friends.

Hyde was wanted by them almost as much as White, for Hyde had sent into freedom 517 fugitives. Since they could not find Hyde, they arrested several other abolitionists in the village, and, in the middle of the night, started back toward the Ohio River.

The alarm went out. A hundred men tumbled out of bed, grabbed their rifles, jumped on their horses, and started in pursuit. They caught up with the deputies and scattered them in all directions. Some deputies tried to break into sleeping houses to hide, but the angry citizens of Mechanicsburg captured several and carried them off to jail in Springfield, Ohio.

The district court in Springfield, acting for the federal authorities, released the deputies. Without a moment's hesitation, Ohio announced that such an act was a violation of states' rights, and the whole issue was thrown onto a national scale. The governor of Ohio, Salmon P. Chase, and the President struck a compromise: the cases against *everyone* would be dropped.

The proslavery newspaper, the Cincinnati *Enquirer*, said this was "a declaration of war on the part of Chase and his abolition crew against the United States courts. Let war come, the sooner the better."

The cry for war was heard more and more often. "Invasion" was frequently on the lips of militant abolitionists. *Go in and bring them out! Tear out the roots of slavery!*

Alexander Ross was a Canadian, a distinguished doctor, an authority on ornithology, entomology, ichthyology. He was the author of several books, and later he was knighted by the emperor of Russia and the kings of Italy, Portugal, Saxony, and Greece for his scientific discoveries. But he was most proud of his work as an "invader."

In Richmond, Virginia, he spoke to a secret meeting of forty-two slaves, meeting in the home of a colored preacher. He explained how the Underground worked and the need to strike a blow for freedom.

Nine slaves promptly said they wished to strike such a blow. Ross gave each a few dollars, a pocket compass, a knife, a pistol, as much food as he could carry, and careful instructions.

Those nine reached freedom safely, and so Ross traveled into the deeper South, where the word and ways of freedom were needed even more. In Georgia he fitted out eleven slaves for the long journey to the North.

No one suspected him. He was to everyone but the slave a bona fide ornithologist. He wandered into fields and woods looking for his specimens—but the specimens were usually human.

From Georgia he went on to South Carolina, and from there to Mississippi. In Vicksburg, the quiet, well-bred scientist lived with a private family, made frequent trips to a neighboring plantation, and always returned with a fine botanical specimen which he eagerly displayed.

Slaves invariably disappeared soon after, but no one

connected their disappearance with him. He had developed a code which fugitives committed to memory. It led them safely from station to station. For example, Meadville, Pennsylvania, was known by the number 10; Seville, Ohio, by 20; Medina, Ohio, by 27. Cleveland was called "hope"; Sandusky, "sunrise"; Detroit, "midnight"; and the ports of entry into Canada were all bursts of praise. Windsor was "Glory to God"; Port Stanley, "God be Praised." So "Helpers at work at midnight" was merely a poetic phrase except to the slave who held the key.

To slaveowners, men like Ross—and he was not alone in this reckless work—were natural enemies. Such men could be shot down without questions asked, or they could be lynched. Ross escaped both fates. But 1857 was not a happy year in which to live. Border warfare flared up again and again, with slave catchers making raids into free states only to be driven back by armed abolitionists.

In Congress, the excited distrust of Buchanan and the men who surrounded him never allowed the battle to relax between the small body of antislavery men and the large body of those dedicated to slavery.

Northern men were as nervous as Southern men. Radical abolitionists were stirring up new enemies among the Republicans who felt their own gradual methods were the only means to end slavery. The country was prostrate under a terrible depression which had begun in August 1857, and antislavery efforts to link the deadening economic effects of slavery to the plight of the poverty-stricken Northern factory workers were not successful.

English workingmen tried this year to open the eyes of Americans to the link between black slavery and white exploitation. A blasting protest signed by eighteen hundred English workmen was sent across the Atlantic. It attempted to trace the vicious circle of American slavery, American cotton planters, and British millowners who kept wages low in order to meet the competition of the American "wage slaves" in American mills.

"Wage slaves" was also a popular slogan among Southerners. Dozens of articles were written comparing the terrible plight of the Northern workingman to the secure life of the slave.

The South of these late 1850's was filled with old clichés freshened up for a new generation. "Why talk about black slavery when white men are the victims of—wages?" "Here in the slaveland is no poverty, no almshouses, no jails."

Never before in the history of the South was every crack and cranny of thinking plugged up as it was now. Politics, scientific investigations, historical analysis, the Bible, popular literature—everything was used in a vast propaganda to bolster a dying system.

The slave republics of Greece and Rome became the great classic examples which the United States should follow. Slavery became "an institution of divine appointment."

Dr. S. A. Cartwright of Mississippi blossomed into a man of great influence in the South because he produced many ingenious theories "proving" by "scientific" investigation that the desire to run away on the part of a slave was due to a form of mental illness called drapetomania, common to Negroes and to cats. He also "discovered" that the Negro brain froze in a cold climate, inducing insanity, and so he urged, out of kindness to the Negro, that he be kept in the South. In addition to all this, he offered interesting "confirmation scientifically arrived at" that the Negro was identical with the serpent who had tempted Eve, the word *Nachash* having been wrongly translated "snake" instead of "Negro."

George Fitzhugh of Virginia also had a tremendous impact on Southern thinking. He was a brilliant man and a student of modern economics, and he offered a blueprint for the future.

He urged a form of government in which everyone, black and white, would be enslaved, all competition abolished, all property and all manpower put under the absolute control of the government. This system he recommended for the entire country except the South, where things would remain as they were, "a paradise of the white race."

He sent out ringing and carefully worded appeals, painting a grim picture of "surrender to socialism and communism—no church, no law, free love, free lands, free women and free children" if the abolition dream were fulfilled.

How simply the whole agitation could have been stated:

"We do not intend to lose one billion dollars' worth of human property."

At the end of 1857 a final effort was made by Buchanan to have Kansas admitted as a slave state. But Congress rejected the plan he offered. The slave power had built its future on Kansas and lost—in spite of the Dred Scott decision. Now it became a matter of salvaging, recouping, and growing strong again.

Unless this were indeed the end. . . .

The Republicans began to move into position, and Abraham Lincoln, the Republican nominee for senator from Illinois, spoke some words that sent a chill through the South.

He reiterated that all men are "created free and equal."

Even some of his friends begged him to tone down this "radicalism."

But Lincoln was an antislavery man. He was not an abolitionist, but he was opposed to slavery and would do all he could to bring it to an orderly end.

Many of the things he was saying were essentially conservative. Why should they send a chill? "A house divided against itself cannot stand. I believe this government cannot endure permanently half slave and half free." Antislavery men had been saying this since the Constitution was drafted, and slave masters had been saying it year after year.

Yet it was quite true that no Northerner made it a political issue if he had supreme ambitions for the future. This Lincoln—what did he want in the future?

Stephen Douglas and Lincoln agreed to debate his points, Douglas hoping to cripple the Republicans and Lincoln hoping to catch the ears of the country.

In the light of torches in public squares, in the light of the sun on fair grounds, down a line of Illinois towns stretching from border to border, Douglas challenged Lincoln to say that he was not advocating the end of the Union. Douglas had a senatorship to hold and Lincoln one to gain. People coming in wagonloads over the dusty roads, in trains, by horseback had to decide between them.

Douglas expected to make short work of the slow lean man who contested his Illinois power.

The whole country listened hard. Lincoln talked the way the average man talked, no frills, no fancy words. In Illinois, the people cast their votes, and Lincoln won by a popular majority, but Douglas won the control of the state legislature, and in those days the legislature decided the winner.

All Lincoln said was, "I am after larger game."

That year the Republicans won Pennsylvania, and they made gains east and west. They promised Northern industry support and a protective tariff. That was all the South needed to confirm its alarm!

For thirty years the South had fought against such a tariff. Although the South was dependent on the North for nearly everything from food to a university education, yet Southern extremists immediately set up a fearful cry.

Sever all relations with the North. Develop a direct trade with English mills. Build our own railroads to the Pacific. Legalize the slave trade [which was flourishing

142

illegally] *for, without the revival of the slave trade, the plantation system is doomed.*

The slave power was perfectly aware of all the forces operating against it, both within and without. At the twenty-fifth anniversary of the New England Antislavery Society, terrible and challenging words were spoken. "Is slavery destined as it began in blood so to end? Seriously and solemnly, we say it seems as if it were."

The antislavery ranks were worn to a thin bone. How much more could the colored and white abolitionists say or do? Through them, the North had learned of the moral and physical horror of slavery. If the North did not now act by peaceful legislation, it must act by force. It was a period of painful waiting, of deep silences, of wondering.

Many of the old abolitionists were dying. Five of the signers of Garrison's Declaration of Sentiments had gone within the year, and they were men badly needed. Everyone seemed waiting for something. The whole country seemed waiting.

It was a midnight of misty vapors when the train from the west, bound for Baltimore, slowed up at Harpers Ferry, Virginia, before crossing the river. The conductor, looking down from the car, could not believe his eyes when he saw men with rifles. For six hours, the train was not allowed to proceed. It was many more hours before the crackle of telegraph wires spread the word—"the slaves have risen up! John Brown has seized Harpers Ferry!"

Old John Brown had tried to light a fuse which would

burn down the length of the South and raise a Negro insurrection such as no one had seen before. But he had miscalculated. In this western part of the state were few slaves to set a light to such a fuse. By nightfall, troops were closing in on the town, and the tremendous, improbable, but fervent plan of Brown had failed.

Every newspaper reported on his trial in full detail. One might be frightened by the means he took, but every man and woman of antislavery conscience heard his defense with deep emotion.

. . . "Had I interfered in the manner which I admit in behalf of the rich, the powerful, the intelligent, every man in this court would have deemed it an act worthy of reward. But I interfered in behalf of God's despised poor. I did not wrong but right."

The day he was hanged, church bells tolled in the North, and Longfellow wrote in his diary, "This will be a great day in our history, the date of a new revolution." Wendell Phillips said, "Marvellous old man, he has abolished slavery in Virginia. True, the slave is still there. So, when the tempest uproots a pine in your hills, it looks green for months. Still it is timber, not a tree. John Brown has loosened the roots of the slave system. It only breathes —it does not live—hereafter."

It would be false to suggest that the North was unanimous in its feeling for Brown. Many were as horrified as were the Southerners, but the Southerners made little distinction between them.

To the South, every bell that tolled for John Brown proclaimed "the approbation of insurrection and servile war." Southern newspapers saw the North and the South divided at Harpers Ferry and standing in battle array on either side of the Potomac River.

Northern travelers brought back word from Virginia and the Carolinas of being stopped by patrols and forced to give an exact reason for their presence. Agents of Northern businesses were attacked and beaten up.

Some men began to ask, "Is this Union worth fighting for?"

The abolitionists were not war lovers. Over and over they had faced the fact that the economic structure that had risen out of slavery might bring about its own downfall in blood, but they took no pleasure in it.

Blood and chaos and despair—it seemed a terrible price to pay for the end of slavery.

Along the Ohio River, the tension lay deep and poignant. The "trains" coming up the river carried their heavy loads with the tense expectancy that any trip might be the last.

Farther West in Kansas the conductors had become men of daring, sharp on the trigger, and the Railroad was coming to the surface, a challenge to open conflict.

In the East, the familiar scenes were being re-enacted so many times that one hardly had time to take precautions.

15

CHARLESTON was unbearably hot in April, 1860. The delegates to the Democratic National Convention hired a hall and slept in rows on cots. The delegates from the North had an opportunity to see in operation that system for which they had, time after time, given their political lives. After ten o'clock at night, they were told, they could not play their band music, as drums might be mistaken for the alarm signal of a slave uprising.

One issue at the convention was simplicity itself, as far as the Southerners were concerned: Stephen Douglas must be defeated. On Douglas' shoulders lay the responsibility for the loss of Kansas and all the territories of the West, for tariff proposals that would strangle the South. If by a wild mischance Douglas were given the nomination, the Southern delegates would split open the party.

Two days of fierce debate, and the Northern delegates

agreed to most of the proposals. Yet they refused to guarantee complete party control to the planters, and even without Douglas the split came with a mighty roar.

The Republicans met in May in Chicago in a blaze of excitement. William Seward was bound to be the nominee. No one knew exactly what happened, but when the votes were counted, Abraham Lincoln was cheered as the next President of the United States.

The abolitionists did not know Lincoln. They waited and watched. In Congress, the slave power struck boldly to gain what it could before the inevitable climax. An effort was made to annex Cuba in order to balance the loss of free lands in the West, but the effort was defeated. Buchanan, however, straightened the balance somewhat by vetoing the Homestead Bill which made land cheaply available to those who would cultivate and live on it. Antislavery men had considered a Homestead Bill essential to encourage free-labor men to continue moving out to the West.

The slave power defeated bill after bill for the benefit of Northern industry. They completely tied the Democratic Party to a slave economy, protected and extended by the Constitution. They introduced measures that would have bound farmers and mechanics to complete dependence on the slave power. They attempted to hamstring Northern capital so that it could not be used in any fashion against slavery. The Republicans said that power, slipping from Democratic hands, was driving them crazy.

Meanwhile the two halves of the Democratic convention were meeting separately. In Baltimore, the Northern Democrats nominated Douglas for President. He was given, as a desperate measure to attract Southern votes, a Georgia running mate who had taken for his personal slogan the motto of the slave power: "Capital should own labor."

The Southern Democrats, meeting again in Charleston, nominated John C. Breckinridge of Kentucky for President.

To the slave power, this disastrous split of the Democratic Party seemed of little importance as long as the prerogatives of slavery were protected. The South was again at a high point of prosperity. One hundred fifty million dollars was the approximate value that year of the slave trading. The illegal slave trade continued, and ships bearing Negroes seized in Africa were putting in to every harbor, including New York.

Against this figure stood another figure, one million dollars, the annual value of slaves who escaped. Both slaveowner and Railroad men believed that this figure was, in actual fact, very much higher.

In this crucial year, 1860, slave insurrections blazed in every Southern state. In almost every case, poor white men joined the slaves.

Slaves and whites were arrested, beaten, and hanged from Texas to Virginia. On many plantations, strikes took place—slaves laid down their tools and refused to work until conditions were made better.

148

The Southern stations of the underground line were now operating as efficiently as the Northern stations. Alexander Ross was still distributing his compasses and directions and would continue to do so until the guns of Fort Sumter put an end to his work.

Thomas Garrett, writing to Philadelphia, told of the more frequent visits of Harriet Tubman and allowed a sense of mounting danger to creep into his reports.

"There is now much more risk than there has been for many months, yet as it is Harriet who seems to have a special angel to guide her on her journeys of mercy, I continue to have hope."

In Cleveland, Ohio, assistance to over a hundred fugitives a month was reported. In New York, the figure ran into the thousands.

In this atmosphere of alarm and crisis, the presidential campaign blazed through the states. Lincoln, the unknown; Lincoln, the man with no record; Lincoln, the homespun wit, had to bear the Republicans to victory.

The abolitionists still distrusted Lincoln. Who was he? He said too many contradictory things. Only Frederick Douglass, among the abolition leaders, gave to Lincoln the support of his eloquent voice.

Northern towns rang with speeches, with the tramping of torchlight parades and the shouting of jubilant Republicans. Southern towns echoed to the drilling and parading of blue-cockaded "minutemen." Lincoln's name did not appear on a single ballot in the South. "To subject the slavocracy to popular plebiscites means revolution and the subversion of all law and order," wrote a Southern newspaper.

The conservatives of the North were in a panic. The Republicans were not yet in office, but the South was already arming! Many businessmen and financiers saw this man from the West, this Lincoln, as a dangerous revolutionary, and they formed desperate coalitions to keep him from victory.

Appeasements and concessions were offered publicly and in Congress, and "the unconditional and early repeals of personal liberty laws"—those laws that protected the Northern Negro—were promised. Massachusetts, New York, Pennsylvania called up their respectable mobs and turned them loose against the abolitionists to show that a change in party did not need to be a change in anything else.

But it was now too late to turn back the clock. On the sixth of November, in an atmosphere of unbearable tension which the bonfires, the shouting, and the singing did not conceal, Abraham Lincoln was elected President.

For the first time, the abolitionists felt a wave of excitement. "The slave has chosen a President of the United States," cried Wendell Phillips. "Lincoln is in place, Garrison in power."

To the South there was no extravagance in these words. The abolitionists and the slave power had always understood each other perfectly.

By the next day, the newspapers, the politicians, the preachers of the South were calling for secession conventions, and the governor of South Carolina was threatening to arm ten thousand men.

Northern trade with the South ended that day. The stock exchange went crazy. From two to three hundred million dollars in Southern debt stood on the Northern books. All loans were called in by the banks.

The poor old man, Buchanan, who sat in the White House, could only wring his hands. Lincoln, with *his* hands tied until his inauguration many months hence, could only repeat over and over the sanctity of the Union and refuse to be drawn into hysterical compromise.

It was popularly believed that Buchanan's State of the Union speech, delivered when Congress convened in December, had been written by Jefferson Davis.

It was a sermon on the sinfulness and folly of free states. It blamed the North for all the country's difficulties. It chided the South for not abiding by the choice of the majority, but at the same time it maintained the South's right to "revolutionary resistance to the government" if its slave property was further endangered.

The speech pleased neither the North nor the South. No one was soon to forget the wild confusion of that Congress, the bewilderment, the frantic devices to avoid catastrophe. Resolutions were passed—eleven one day, eighteen another day, twenty-four soon after—all designed to ride the storm. Everyone felt the coldness of desperation, and Lincoln could do nothing for he was not yet President. The weeks dragged toward the fourth of March, 1861.

"The truth is," Alexander Stephens wrote from Georgia, "our leaders do not desire to continue [the Union] on any terms." Stephens had been, for many years, a congressman from Georgia and he would soon be the Vice President of the Confederacy.

Down in Charleston harbor, Major Anderson, the commander of Fort Moultrie, was besieged, and the new million-dollar Fort Sumter, nearby, was ungarrisoned. He sent desperate pleas to Washington, but Floyd, the Secretary of War, held out no hope. Time would take care of Major Anderson, for in Charleston, a secession convention was driving hard toward the end of the Union.

Major Anderson, a Southern man but also an officer determined to do his duty, heard the bells of Charleston. He heard the shouting voices come across the harbor: "The Union is dissolved!" He saw the state flag appear at every window, and he knew that he must decide his own position.

He transferred his command secretly at night to Fort Sumter, on an island, and therefore easier to defend. Charleston was furious, for the secessionists claimed all the forts. The other forts were promptly seized and commissioners were sent to Buchanan to insist that Anderson be recalled.

Only Buchanan's Secretary of State stood with poor Anderson. A merchant ship was dispatched with supplies and two hundred reinforcements. Charleston opened fire, and the ship withdrew.

The seceding states were going rapidly now, although

in every state legislature a few staunch Unionists put their lives in danger by protesting against secession.

Mississippi, Florida, Alabama had gone out of the Union—although Alabama went so reluctantly that the Unionists were denounced as "traitors and rebels." In Georgia a long convention battle was being fought. "Security committees" threatened the stubborn delegates who refused to vote for secession, and these delegates resisted up to the final vote. Pickens County continued to fly the Stars and Stripes for six weeks after secession was declared.

No further efforts were made to relieve Sumter, for no one would send the order. When the Secretary of the Treasury, on his own account, sent a wire to the captain of a revenue cutter off Louisiana, "If any man attempts to haul down the American flag, shoot him on the spot," the message was not delivered.

People said Lincoln looked like an old man. Sitting in Springfield, Illinois, without authority or power, he could only watch a house divided, fall.

In the South, business was at a standstill, the price of slaves had been slashed in half. The border states were unknown quantities—were they for or against the Union?

In Montgomery, Alabama, the secessionists were meeting, and there they formed themselves into a Confederacy. They adopted a constitution, modeled on the only one that Americans knew but with the word *slave* introduced where it had been conspicuously omitted by the

Founding Fathers. Jefferson Davis would be their first President, Alexander Stephens, their Vice President.

In Davis' first speech he said, "Our new government is . . . resting upon the great truth that the Negro is not equal to the white man, and subordination to the superior race his natural and normal condition. This, our new government, is the first in the history of the world based on this great physical, philosophical, and moral truth."

To the North, each climax was worse than the preceding one. Shall the seceding states be allowed to go in peace? as some urged, or shall any concession—every concession—be made? as mass meetings in New York were demanding. Could the North live without the South? Could the South live without the North?

(Fugitives coming up the long underground roads said that all the Negroes knew "Marse Linco'm is a-comin' and all de slaves are free!")

Lincoln left his home in Springfield for the slow journey to Washington. Down in Charleston harbor, Major Anderson still held out with his sixty men. Sumter was now a test of nerves. Whoever had the greatest patience would win the fort.

Lincoln's train was making a slow, triumphant progress across the North. Addressing crowds at every stop, he was forever talking about the Union as though no Confederacy existed.

He spent four days in Washington (before he took his oath) trying to protect what he could of a disintegrating government. Virginia, Tennessee, North Carolina, Arkansas still trembled just outside the Confederacy.

The fourth of March dawned, with armed companies marching through the streets. All night the Senate had been debating an amendment to the Constitution, an amendment which would prohibit, forever, the abolition of slavery by Congressional action. If it passed, it would become the Thirteenth Amendment.

. . . When, four years later, the Thirteenth Amendment was added to the Constitution, it gave by an irony of history complete freedom to the Negro.

16

IN his inaugural address, Lincoln said that the Union could not be broken except by the express consent of the entire country.

He held out the hand of friendship to the South, although he did not compromise with his principles. Many were greatly cheered. Even Garrison was moved by "the manly courage" of Lincoln, and he agreed that the South had been permitted a wide avenue back into the Union— if one wanted the South back. But events were moving faster than conciliation.

Lincoln determined to relieve Sumter by sending an armed ship under convoy. Sumter lay in a steel ring of 7000 men and 140 cannon. Yet the convoy was detached on Seward's orders—he was the new Secretary of State— and the ship, sent by Lincoln, stood off the bar of Charleston harbor, unprotected. All along the Battery, men and women in gay clothes crowded to look out to sea where the Yankee ship lay against the horizon. Would Sumter surrender now? The United States flag flying over it told no tales.

In Charleston, the night was wild with rumors. The streets were brightly lighted. Each horse that galloped by came—who knows?—from Davis or from Beauregard, on whose joint commands lay Southern honor.

Two o'clock, three o'clock, four o'clock, a faint dawn was showing. Along the streets, the people moved again toward the Battery to see which flag was flying over Sumter. The night had brought no change. Perhaps today . . . perhaps . . . at first many thought the sudden roar was thunder, then they realized that it was a gun. A second roar, and Sumter replied.

And thus the Civil War began.

The cannonading lasted for two days, and crowds came in carriages to watch from the sea wall. At last Sumter fell.

Ten days passed. Virginia—in or out of the Union?— hung in the balance. In her secession convention, the Union men were holding fast against the secessionists. The hours were agonizing.

It seemed for a terrible moment that every army officer was a Southerner and that Washington was completely unguarded. Cassius Clay, the abolitionist from Kentucky, and Jim Lane, one of the abolitionists from Kansas, were scouring the city for volunteers who would shoulder a gun, patrol the streets, guard the White House, till the Massachusetts boys, the boys from Pennsylvania got there.

In Virginia, no one outside the convention hall knew what the vote for or against secession had been. Maybe secession lost, for the men from western Virginia had been fighting hard to hold to the Union. The bare announcement of secession did not include the vote. But the fact remained, Virginia had seceded.

Lincoln's face was deeply drawn. The Massachusetts troops had been mobbed coming through Baltimore. He had to hold on to Baltimore, or Washington would be surrounded. He cared only about saving the Union, and the Union was slipping away. Maybe it would become a choice between holding the border states—Maryland, Delaware, Kentucky, Missouri—and keeping the support of the abolitionists.

The abolitionists had really elected him, for it was the old Liberty Party, twenty years before, which had prepared the ground for his election. Some said that he had become, at heart, an abolitionist. But he could not show them his heart. All they could see was his fumbling, his efforts to wheedle, persuade the army recruits that they were fighting not against slavery but for the Union.

The war had to be continually presented as a war to preserve the Union. Lincoln knew he would lose the border states, lose the support of the business and commercial and antiabolition elements in the North if this were not presented simply as a war to preserve the Union.

As indeed it was. But it must never be forgotten that

the only thing which had ever endangered the Union was slavery.

No move escaped Garrison, and Garrison saw something that made him friendly to Lincoln. Garrison puzzled his friends. Had he not always preached disunion? Why was he supporting Lincoln now in a fight to restore the Union? He answered that around Lincoln were bound to gather all the forces of freedom.

Many abolitionists could not agree. Thirty years of persecution made them intensely wary. If this was a war to end slavery, why was emancipation not promptly decreed? Why were black men not given a chance to fight for their freedom? Frederick Douglass and other Negro leaders kept up a tireless agitation for colored regiments.

The administration was greatly disturbed. Since they could not present this war as an antislavery war and hope to keep the North solidly with them, they were uncertain how to deal with the situation. The government refused the Negroes any part.

By May, fugitives were coming through Ohio in carloads. The Underground Railroad had come to the surface, and it was no longer necessary to run the slaves to Canada. In the South the laws were tightening as they had in the days of Vesey and Turner. Many owners drove their slaves into the Deep South; but, wherever they went, the slaves kept the rumors flying about "Mistah Linkum."

This was a terrible year to many antislavery men, for slaves coming for safety into the Union army camps were being turned back to their masters. Many Union officers were conservative, if not indeed proslavery, and they allowed slave agents free access to Union camps to reclaim runaways. Some Northern generals, like Butler and Frémont, were deeply shocked by this. Apart from the inhumanity was the simple fact that every fugitive slave made a drain on the Southern economy and forced one more white man to lay down a gun and pick up a spade. But those in authority insisted the situation was too complicated for such a simple equation.

Butler and Frémont devised techniques for protecting the fugitives, but they were rebuked and their orders countermanded by President Lincoln. This produced a wave of indignation from those who agreed with Butler and Frémont, and a demoralizing confusion followed.

Lincoln explained that emancipation could come only by congressional decree. Abolitionists and Negroes were in despair. They said Lincoln had betrayed them.

Few knew the agony of the man, his desperate conviction that the border states must be held at all costs, his fear of a divided North, his unquenchable concern for human values, his bleak realization that the Union army was losing all the battles.

This first year was a nightmare. In some Northern quarters, Lincoln was hated almost as much as he was in the South. People asked—could the South be beaten? The South sent up a rebel yell: *No!*

In Congress, the debates were violent. Congressmen were beginning to feel the relentless pressure of antislavery constituents. If this were not a war for freedom, then why fight it? Yet "how slow this child of freedom is being born," Sumner exclaimed in despair.

Then suddenly the Sea Islands, off the coast of Georgia, fell to a Union blockade. When the Union soldiers came ashore, the slaves were there to meet them. They had already divided up the plantations among themselves, were assuming full responsibility for law and order, were free men greeting free men.

The soldiers in the blue uniform were touched. Schools were hastily set up, teachers hurried from the North. School was any place covered by a roof, schoolbooks were any bit of printing that lay at hand. Former slaves, eager for learning, were arriving hourly.

The imagination of the North was stirred by this. The abolitionists used it effectively by repeating again and again, "You see—the Negro is our greatest ally. Let black men fight for their freedom."

The government made a tentative gesture. The Southern states were offered compensation if they freed their slaves; it would be their last chance before the government took action. No time limit was set. Yet weak as it was, it could be a straw in the wind.

More straws began to fly. At the end of March, 1862, Union officers were forbidden to use their soldiers as slave catchers. In April slavery was abolished in the District of Columbia. In July, after it had a stormy passage through Congress, Lincoln signed a bill freeing slaves who came within the Union lines, emancipating slave soldiers, and decreeing liberty in general to all rebel-owned slaves who sought it. This was a sweeping but entirely ineffectual confiscation act. Five days later an order guaranteed wages to all slaves who came within the Union lines.

These developments and assurances filtered through the patrol lines, and the flight of slaves increased to great mass movements. One million dollars worth of slaves was saying good-by to North Carolina weekly, according to a Confederate general, and eastern Georgia sent an urgent plea to the Confederate government to do something to halt the flight of property worth from twelve to fifteen million dollars.

A greater uprising of slaves was going on than the imagination could grasp. This was an uprising of bondmen, like the Jews in Egypt, taking their masters' possessions and leaving the fields and granaries of the South, leaving the labor battalions, and pouring into the Union lines. What good were laws, pleas to loyalty, night riders? Five hundred thousand men, women, and children, crossing the Union lines, was the answer to that.

Emancipation was in the air. For the first time, Lincoln was talking about it to his Cabinet. Agitation for freedom was growing all over the North. Church delegations drew up petitions and presented them to Lincoln. He asked for more petitions. He said the will of the people must be felt. More petitions poured in. To many Northerners, the issue had become simple: emancipation and a quick peace, or slavery and a long war.

All summer Lincoln listened—to a Congress restless with the Maryland, Delaware, Kentucky, Missouri representatives, many of them slaveholding Democrats, and equally restless with its indecisive Republicans. Lincoln listened to the voice of Garrison and Phillips and Frederick Douglass and Thaddeus Stevens, of antislavery societies, of wavering men suddenly determined to "Arm the Negro!"

In Louisiana, General Butler was holding the area around New Orleans. He sent out a call to the free colored people, "Defend the Union!" In South Carolina, General Hunter, who held Port Royal, went ahead and enlisted a regiment of freed slaves. The tide was moving fast.

In Congress, the opposition grew more wordy, but antislavery retorts beat it down. Antislavery was becoming respectable. Faltering legislation was passed that permitted the enlistment of five thousand Negroes.

Black men flocked to the recruiting offices. Within a month, the First Regiment of Louisiana Native Guards, under the Union General Butler, went onto the battlefield.

Thomas Wentworth Higginson, a long-time abolitionist, was in command of a Union regiment in South Carolina. General Butler sent him an urgent message to see what he could do to make soldiers out of the slaves pouring into the Union lines.

Higginson looked over the recruits. He knew all the dangers and the responsibilities. If these black soldiers

163

were a failure, the proslavery forces in the North would be delighted. He was a hot-headed, impetuous, daring, utterly courageous man who loved freedom. He liked what he saw here. The recruits were all as black as night. Not a mulatto in the group. That's what he wanted. Negroes whose good qualities could not be explained away by any touch of white blood.

He squatted down beside a Negro guerrilla who had just been carried in with serious wounds. "Did you think this was more than you bargained for?" he asked him. The man rolled his eyes to look at Higginson. "I been thinkin', mas'r, *it's jess what I went for.*"

Raw! They were more raw than a farm hand who had drilled with a plow handle, but Higginson had what he wanted. The First South Carolina Volunteers, colored, went into action within six weeks, and covered themselves with glory.

Missouri, a slave state within the Union, was troubled. Her slaves were melting over the border into Iowa, Illinois, Kansas. When the third Negro regiment took to the field, it was the First Kansas Colored, and most of the soldiers had taken the underground line out of Missouri. Nearly half Missouri's Negro population had vanished out of the state. Finally, in a grim effort to keep what she had left, Missouri asked permission to include Negroes in her quota of Union troops.

But where was emancipation?

17

ONE day in September, 1862, the telegraph wires all over the North began to hum. The message coming over the wires carried the words which had been so eagerly and desperately wanted by the Negro and his friends. The message stopped men in their tracks.

"On the first day of January in the year of our Lord one thousand eight hundred and sixty three, all persons held as slaves within any state . . . *the People thereof then in rebellion* . . . shall be henceforward and forever free."

It was the promise of emancipation.

The north had gone from one lost battle to another. The war was unpopular. Men avoided the draft as best they could. There had even been draft riots in some of the larger Northern cities. Lincoln had not dared to make so vivid and essential a promise of emancipation —which many in the North would not support—until some military victory raised the hope that the North would win. The small Union victory at Antietam was of no great consequence, but Lincoln seized upon it, for he knew he could not wait any longer.

Surprise and rejoicing and confusion rose wherever two or three people met together. A friend calling to congratulate Garrison found him curiously silent. He was disturbed, he admitted. Why had the President not included the border states in his message? Although the border states—Kentucky, Missouri, Delaware, Maryland —might be technically within the Union, nevertheless they held thousands of slaves. How could the proclamation be *enforced* in enemy territory, he asked; or, if the slaves attempted to act upon it themselves, how could they be protected from their masters? Why did the President leave the Confederacy three months—from September till January—in which to make its own freedom proclamation, on its own terms (and there were rumors that they planned to do this) and thus win the moral support of Europe which was already half sympathetic to the side of the South?

Any of these things could happen between September and January and could shift the whole balance away from emancipation.

Privately Garrison and Phillips spread their caution to inexperienced and excited friends who wished promptly to disband the societies and end all their work.

166

They reminded them that a proclamation of freedom had only moral force. It could not actually free the slaves.

The next three months were tense and nervous times. Rumors spread that slave masters planned to sell their slaves to Cuba or spirit them off to South America. Fears deepened that Lincoln might weaken under the angry protests of the Southern papers and the wholesale resignations of conservative Union officers influenced by General George B. McClellan, whom Lincoln had dismissed. He might, for expediency's sake, not confirm the proclamation in January as he had promised.

But the proclamation was already spreading by grapevine through the slave South. Confederate units were being detached from the army, where they were badly needed, and being sent to fight rebellious slaves, and open Union sympathy was being expressed by poor white men in the South.

Events hung in a strange balance for those three months. Democrats won in local elections, and this frightened the supporters of Lincoln. On the stock exchange prices were falling, and in the army troops were deserting and enlistments were lagging.

As the year drew to a close, the abolitionists realized that they *had* to be Lincoln men, heart and soul, in order to give him the strength to withstand their common enemy. The intellectual men, like Lowell and Longfellow (who long ago had come to the side of freedom) and like Hawthorne and Oliver Wendell Holmes (who had held aloof from any commitment) now found themselves exhilarated by the urgency of these times.

New Year's Eve, 1861, the eve of emancipation, assumed almost a religious fervor. Jubilee celebrations were arranged, for Lincoln had not weakened under pressure and in a few more hours the words of the proclamation would become a fact.

In London several thousand workingmen set aside this New Year's Eve as a night in which to denounce slavery. In the North New Year's Eve was a watch night in all the colored churches.

Tomorrow—would tomorrow never come?—tomorrow that carried the end of shackles, the end of slave whips. White friends were holding the night-long vigil with Negroes. In every city of the North they met together to wait together.

A thousand memories filled these hours until the proclamation was reaffirmed. . . . A man who had only stumps for legs had hidden in the swamps by day, dragged himself along by night, but he had found freedom! An old woman had gathered a ball and chain into her hands and fled to the woods to freedom. Eliza and a thousand like her had taken the long road back into the slavelands and brought their families out to freedom. Antislavery men had maintained their watches along the Ohio River, and all the named and unnamed heroes had hurried their black passengers along a road which no one ever saw, which ran beyond the reach of human greed into a strange brightness called freedom. Harriet

Tubman had whistled her message outside slave cabins and Thomas Garrett had written in a calm hand, "Look for twelve more of God's poor tomorrow night." Garrison had stumbled through a respectable mob and smiled because he saw something they did not see—he foresaw this night and these vigils, and black and white holding hands like brothers. . . .

In Boston, the night watches were to last through the day at Tremont Temple until the proclamation itself came over the wires. Everyone expected the message to come by noon. But by noon no word had come, and the afternoon wore on. Nerves tightened. Messengers had been established between the telegraph offices and the platform of the temple.

The people sang. The orchestra played Mendelssohn's *Hymn of Praise*. Beethoven's Fifth Symphony, Handel's *Hallelujah Chorus*. Darkness fell. Friends tried not to look at each other for fear their own courage would fail. What was happening in Washington? Soon they would have to go home, and how would they fill the silence when these encouraging hymns and this music were still?

They started to sing again, swelling their voices more resolutely. At that moment a man ran down the aisles. First they heard his voice indistinctly, and then they heard it in a shout. "Over the wires—*it's coming over the wires now!*"

The glad cry that rose should have lifted the walls of the building. People were weeping, singing, pounding out their applause. All their fears and suspicions of Lincoln went roaring to the roof as they cheered nine mighty times for him, and then looked about for their own great men to cheer.

Garrison—where was Garrison? There he was, up in the gallery, and they called out his name, and, as he rose, they hurled three more tremendous cheers to him. And then someone pointed again to the gallery, and another name ran from tongue to tongue—Mrs. Stowe!—Mrs. Stowe!

She stood there for a moment, her bonnet slightly askew, her eyes filled with tears, but smiling, bowing —"the little woman who started this great war," as Lincoln had called her—and the whole audience came to its feet.

The full proclamation was brought into the hall. There it was ". . . henceforward and forever free . . ." The thousands of voices rose as one, singing:

> *Sound the loud timbrel o'er Egypt's dark sea!*
> *Jehovah has triumph'd,—his people are free!*

Garrison and Phillips might still warn against the incomplete nature of this emancipation, might remind the country that in the border states eight hundred and thirty thousand slaves had not been included in the proclamation, that in the rebellious states the federal government had no power to enforce the proclamation. That it was a moral statement only. But to the average Northerner freedom for the slave had come. It took a long time to realize that many more steps were necessary before slavery was brought to a final end.

However, slaves in the border states waited for nothing. They heard the words *forever free,* and many simply packed up and left. Kentucky lost thirty thousand. Missouri once more complained that wagon loads of their slaves were rattling into Union lines from every town in the state.

Lincoln authorized the raising of Negro troops. They were desperately needed. The famous Fifty-Fourth Massachusetts swung on its way in February, and the Fifty-Fifth followed soon on its heels—part of those two hundred thousand Negro soldiers who were, by Lincoln's testimony, to turn the tide for the Union.

Garrison stood with tears in his eyes, on the very corner past which he had been dragged on that memorable day in October, 1835. He watched the Fifty-Fourth march past, the fair-haired young Robert Shaw, of a famous abolition family, riding at its head, and he listened to the song that the rich voices were rolling back, rank upon rank:

John Brown's body lies a-mouldering in the grave,
His soul goes marching on.

The abolitionists knew that their work was by no means done. Many Northern generals hated the proclamation and undermined it whenever they could. The Confederacy gave orders that Union officers, taken captive, were to be treated as inciters to insurrection, that

Negro soldiers, captured, were to be shot as rebellious slaves.

The old Underground Railroad people transferred their work to those points along the Mississippi River where fugitives were concentrating, to the camps, the settlements, and the schools set up behind Union lines. Many of the slaves were injured and starving, but their morale was high.

The Union general, Ulysses S. Grant, commanding in this area gave them every support, and he assigned to a young chaplain of a volunteer Ohio regiment, named John Eaton, the task of bringing order out of his mass of human woe, of combating sickness and providing food and shelter. The Ohio River had seen much Negro misery, but the sufferings of these fugitives were more terrible than anything that had been seen before. The abolitionists worked twenty-four hours a day, but the law was now on their side; hope was now legal.

The war had still to be won and a wartime proclamation given the status of law. The next two years were harsh and violent. Draft rioters, traitors, terrible division in the North—a civil war within the Civil War—made victory seem heartbreakingly distant.

But the average Negro did not know this. The Negro leaders could not afford to acknowledge it. The Negro soldiers fought with conspicuous courage and spread the word of emancipation along the swamps and by-ways of the South, by the underground telegraph; and the extent and exactness of information owned by the slaves was the marvel of every Union officer.

The Confederacy itself was by no means the solid structure that later romantics made it. Poor whites in the Appalachians—those mountains ranging from Virginia to Alabama—fought a constant guerrilla warfare against the Confederacy. White men forged passes for Negroes in Richmond and in Savannah. They organized rings that smuggled slaves to freedom, and they ran an "underground railroad" that carried Union prisoners from Southern prison camps to the North.

When it became clear at last that the North would win this war, the friends of the Negro turned their full efforts toward the immediate future. The hatred of the Negro must be conquered in the North. He must be given full legal protection.

On Lincoln's desk and on the desks of Cabinet members and senators were full reports from the plantation lands occupied by Northern troops. Land cultivation showed a profit when owned and handled by Negroes. John Eaton, who was now head of the Freedmen's Bureau, pointed to the remarkable success of those freedmen—mostly Jefferson Davis' former slaves—who had leased tracts of land on the ten-thousand-acre Davis plantation in Mississippi. Self-government in the form of Negro sheriffs and judges appointed to have jurisdiction over certain districts had been established. Negro troops had been assigned to protect the colony, and much of the land was worked on a cooperative basis.

Of the hundred thirteen thousand fugitives under Eaton's care the previous year, sixty two thousand were now entirely self-supporting. "Those who were cheated and abused last year," he wrote, "will hardly be so this year. They who had contracts desire to learn to read them. They who have once been cheated in changing money desire to be able to calculate. We can see the wants, desires and hopes of civilized life struggling within them."

Lincoln agreed. Help must be given. But he wanted the country to speak first. He urged the antislavery men to send delegations to Congress—strong delegations who could hold onto a congressman's lapel and not let it go until he had listened.

So delegations swept in, staid, dignified, from Boston, New York, Philadelphia, Chicago. Lincoln promised a message to Congress.

Lincoln was attempting a balance which was perhaps impossible. To promise the Negro freedom and at the same time mend the break in the Union. To mend the break meant forgetting, as well as possible, these terrible years of war. He tentatively suggested an amnesty to the majority of Southern citizens. The war had still to be won, but it was not too soon to make preparations for peace.

This could mean, of course, that everything would be restored to the past, but under a new name. Many who were cynical said this was what would happen. Slavery would be abolished, but the Negro would still be at the mercy of his old masters. This was a genuine fear unless the Negro were allowed to hold on to the confiscated land which gave him his only security. And equally sinister were the signs that a mere shift in control was taking place—power passing from a dying class of landowners in the South to a rising class of industrialists in the North which had no regard or compassion for either the Negro or the poor white.

Already confiscated plantations were being leased to private contractors in the sections occupied by Union troops, and the failure of the private contractors to pay wages to freedmen was creating a scandal. No solution was being suggested for the deep-lying plight of the poor whites, driven, years ago, by the slave power to small rocky acres; although any Northern businessman with money could buy up vast tracts and run them as he chose. Northern investors were fastening themselves onto the rich lands of the Mississippi Valley where Union troops were in command. Was Northern capital assuming the place of the Southern slave power?

And what about voting, when the war was over? The Negro and the poor white had been disfranchised by the slave power—the Negro because he had no legal standing, the poor white because he did not own sufficient property. Yet the Negro and the poor white had been the friends of the Union.

Lincoln suggested that some be allowed to vote: those who had aided the Union, those who could read and write.

Even these words—entirely unofficial—spread like fire. In southeastern South Carolina, where Union troops had been for a number of years, a call went out in April,

1864, inviting all Union men, irrespective of color, to elect delegates to the presidential convention. Two hundred and fifty men assembled, riding over the hot roads, piercing the heart of that state which had been the center of the slave power—and one hundred fifty of them were colored.

Congressmen began to pay attention to their mail which urged voting rights for Negroes, protection of civil rights in the South. Lincoln might claim that no state could secede, that the Union was only waiting for the erring states to return, but many felt that the bloodiest war in history could not be wiped out so easily.

Many remembered the arrogance, the shouting, the bowie knives of prewar congressmen. Were these same people to be put again in power? What guarantee was offered that the slaveowner mentality had been done away with and that the old rulers would not return, able to juggle emancipation as skillfully as they had juggled slavery?

The Fugitive Slave Law still stood on the statute books.

Seven efforts were made to repeal that law, or at least to weaken it, but the border states, where emancipation did not operate, always protested. In January, 1864, Sumner tried again. Opponents, tangled now in their own opposition, trying to look two ways at once— back to the past, forward to the future—argued automatically against repeal. Then, without warning, they gave in. Within a week, the monstrous law came to an end.

The first step had been taken to make the Emancipation Proclamation something stronger than a military measure without enforcement. Since it had no constitutional standing, a political overturn, a new Congress could restore slavery more quickly than the proclamation had put an end to it. The Congress "radicals" set the wheels spinning that would create a Thirteenth Amendment making slavery in *all* the country illegal and freedom a fact, not a promise.

The summer of 1864 was alive with rumors—of peace, of the impossibility of Lincoln's winning a second term. The Democrats chose McClellan as their nominee, and of course the Republicans renominated Lincoln. George B. McClellan was the former Union general whom Lincoln had dismissed, and he built up a hazy, romantic, but dangerous coalition around him. The voters were confused and weary. The North held on from one thin victory to another, but none was enough to excite a fervent unity behind the President.

Then events began to work for Lincoln. Admiral Farragut had already broken the defenses at Mobile, Alabama. General Sheridan was driving across the Shenandoah Valley in Virginia. On September 1 General Sherman's troops marched into Atlanta. The backbone of the Confederacy had been broken.

Lincoln ordered thanksgiving in all the churches. His supporters leaped into action and whirled the campaign forward on a theme of victory and an early peace. The re-election of Lincoln followed.

The antislavery men used the excitement to shout, "Pass the Thirteenth Admendment! Give the Negro citizenship!"

Pass it, Lincoln pleaded in his December message to Congress.

It came onto the floor of the House in late January. The galleries were packed. No one knew for sure how the voting would go. After an interminable suspense, the Speaker announced that two-thirds of the House had voted to abolish slavery now and forever, here and everywhere.

Pandemonium broke loose. Celebrations shattered the dignity of the House—up and down the staircases on the floor, in the galleries, in the offices of congressmen. Adjournment was carried with shouts, and white and Negro went off to celebrate with cheers and weeping and boundless thanksgiving.

The shoutings spread across the North as the telegraph wires carried the word. Kansas City blazed with lights, cannon boomed. Chicago, Philadelphia swarmed with marchers and speeches and bands. In Boston, one hundred guns were fired and all the church bells were rung.

Garrison went out on the Common to listen, so sweet a sound loosened the tight smile on his face, released a joy in him that sweetened all the bitterness of the past.

The sword was sheathed. Garrison's work was done.

18

NOW surely the work of antislavery men was also done.

But the cautious, the experienced, shook their heads.

The war had not yet been won. The new free Negro was exposed on every side. The millions in the South were free men—but still in prison. The government offered no security for their protection, education, future.

Lincoln had talked a great deal about the task of reconstruction once the war was over. Everyone knew that his great desire was to heal wounds as quickly as possible. The great danger lay in the probability that the men who formerly held power would prove to be the ones most capable of knitting the edges together —and they were the old slave masters.

Sumner in the Senate and Stevens in the House were

not yielding an inch of the black man's rights. Full citizenship meant full and complete security in his person, his property, his opportunities.

Maryland and Missouri abolished slavery with no day of grace to slaveholders, and no compensation. General Lee's estate at Arlington, Virginia, was turned into a freedmen's village, and the plantations of other men who had fought to preserve slavery became schools for colored children.

In Maryland, where Frederick Douglass had been a slave, his son was now teaching in a freedmen's school, and on the Mississippi a new village had sprung up on the land which Jefferson Davis's slaves had bought for their own use.

Negro leaders were urging a convention in Washington to create an ironclad guarantee of Negro suffrage. On February 12, Chief Justice Chase, during a symbolic ceremony designed to "dig the grave for the Dred Scott decision," administered the oath to John S. Rock, the first Negro to be admitted to practice before the Supreme Court.

Lincoln had the abolitionists behind him now as he had never had in the past. It seemed evident to all of them that his heart was set on a fully integrated country and this included the entire well-being of the Negro.

In the early spring of 1865 Fort Sumter and Charleston fell to the Union army, and early in April Richmond fell. Into that battered city, at two o'clock the next afternoon, came the touching unexpected figure of Lincoln and his little son. The President came without announcement, unguarded except for the sailors who rowed him from the boat.

He chose to walk to the new Union headquarters with Tad's hand in his. Down the street he went, matching his long steps to the little boy's, his deeply lined face lifted to the ravages of war and to the few trees showing their spring leaves. No one knew he was in Richmond, yet they came—came from all the side streets, halloing, shouting, dancing around the two Lincolns—and all of them were black.

"Glory! Glory! Glory!" rose in the air. The tall man smiled and waved his hand, and an old Negro with tears rolling down his cheeks said, "May the good Lord bless you, President Linkum."

There, on a warm Virginia street, the man who had fought the war against slavery drove a final golden nail into its casket. He turned toward the old colored man, and taking off his hat, bowed low to him.

The end was swift. At Appomattox, Virginia, on April 9, 1865, Lee surrendered to Grant.

Killing was finished, a Union restored, a nation's honor freed of slavery. Lincoln, very pale, addressed Congress. He urged again that the Southern states be received back as fast as possible and that the "intelligent" Negro, and those who had served in the Union forces, be given an immediate vote.

Building up—building up—this was the great work. He could talk of nothing else. It became his one thought. Canceling the past. Wiping it out.

That was one reason why he sent Garrison and Henry Ward Beecher to Charleston for the raising of the flag over Fort Sumter. The same flag was to go up, the same Major Anderson was to raise it. Garrison, whose life had been demanded by South Carolina, was now to walk the streets unmolested.

Lincoln did not hear about that trip—about the three thousand Negroes who marched shouting with Garrison through the streets, of the two thousand school children who came with garlands and flowers, of the thousands of freedmen who welcomed them to the village of Mitchellville where the first self-governing community of South Carolina freedmen made this a gala day. He did not hear of the speeches of Negro leaders nor of the touching meeting with Lieutenant Garrison who had just returned to camp with twelve hundred ragged refugees, nor of the singing and prayers and rejoicing. He did not hear about these things, for he was dead.

The flag over Fort Sumter had been raised on that fateful day when an assassin's bullet closed the deep dreaming eyes of the President. The abolitionists, bound for Florida and further jubilation, received the word when the boat put into Beaufort. A sickness that ran beyond grief fell upon them. The light of joy was put out. Black faces no longer smiled.

They ordered the ship to return to the North. "The heavens seemed dark," said Beecher, sitting against the rail and looking off across the water. "Nothing was left but God, and His immutable providence, and His decrees. But oh, the sadness of that company, and our night and our day's journey back. We knew only this: the President had been assassinated."

A deep anger settled on the North: a Southerner had done this murder. Now all remnants of the slave power must be totally destroyed.

Yet in the South there was also lamentation. Many white Southerners realized that a man prepared to be their friend had been taken violently from them. In the border states, the bells tolled and mourning bands appeared on many arms. For the Negro, there was despair.

The Vice President, a man from a poor white Tennessee family, Andrew Johnson, took the oath of office.

The friends of the Negro in Congress had faith in him. The friends of the Negro were not demanding revenge (as was later charged against Thaddeus Stevens); they were demanding only a policy that would make clear to the old slavemasters that their power had ended forever.

They were also opposing those Northerners who wished to return the control of the Southern states promptly to the very men who had taken those states out of the Union. They also demanded guarantees that, when education had done its best, the Negro would be admitted into the full rights of citizenship and that, in the interval, he would be protected. In spite of later claims of the South, vengeance was not the desire of the North. The North wished to be assured that the slave power, under another name, would not be restored.

Johnson gave every indication of supporting Lincoln's policy, and even going beyond it. He reassured Negro delegations which came to see him. The only point of disagreement with the "radicals" was the question of confiscation of the great plantations—a step they considered imperative to make democracy work for the landless Negro. Forty acres and a mule—to bring a new economy to the South.

But Johnson betrayed them. That is the word they used. He took the power that belonged only to Congress and issued a North Carolina Proclamation which offered a wide amnesty to former Confederates and excluded all consideration of the Negro in the state constitution. A fight was on.

The next ten years have been the object of much abuse in later histories. We are now beginning to see it with greater clarity.

The South was like any country after a devastating war. Ruin was everywhere. Plantations were wrecked. White men came back to desolate homes. Refugees clogged the roads. A federal army of occupation was the only agency able to enforce some kind of order.

A vague policy for the future was evolving in the

most painful jerks and starts. At last, the people on the bottom, the Negroes, with nothing to lose, took matters into their own hands. They wanted land and they took it. They refused to work until they were given land, or given wages if they worked other men's land.

Many were hungry, more were in rags. Thousands of Negroes were wandering the roads simply because they had never been allowed any freedom of movement before. Or because they were searching for families who, years ago, had been sold into other parts of the South.

No people were ever watched with such remorseless eyes as those freed Negroes of 1865. If a poor black man suddenly insisted on being called "Mister," or if a poor black woman suddenly decided she wanted a red dress and stole it, these acts were seen, not as the groping efforts toward some kind of human dignity, but as the natural irresponsibility of Negroes.

On some of the distant plantations Negroes did not know that freedom had come. In some remote counties they were being re-enslaved. Former slave masters were organizing themselves as terrorists and were hanging Negroes at the slightest provocation.

An Alabaman, sending an urgent testimony to Congress, warned that armed insurrection would follow these terrors which are "particularly flagrant in Alabama and Mississippi," and a Mississippian sent a solemn warning: "If matters are permitted to continue as they now seem likely to be, it needs no prophet to predict a rising on the part of the colored people and a terrible scene of bloodshed and desolation. Nor can anyone blame the Negroes if this proves to be the result. It is sufficient to state that the old overseers are in power again."

Carl Schurz, a Civil War general, and later a famous journalist and a senator, was sent to make an investigation. He wrote:

Some of the planters with whom I talked have expressed their determination to adopt the course which best accords with the spirit of free labor, to make the Negro work by offering him fair inducements, and to extend to him those means of improvement which will make him an intelligent, reliable citizen. . . . I regret to say that these views are confined to a small minority. The popular prejudice is almost as bitterly set against the Negro having the advantages of education as it was when the Negro was a slave. Hundreds of times I heard the old assertion, "Negro education will be the ruin of the South." Wherever I go I hear the people talk in such a way as to indicate that they are unable to conceive of the Negro as possessing any rights at all. The people boast that when they get freedmen's affairs in their own hands, to use their own expression, "the niggers will catch hell."

The fight in Congress between Johnson and the friends of the Negro continued in raw and bitter terms. By presidential decree, Johnson continued to pull back into the Union one seceded state after another, hastily wiping them clean and acceptable. Yet, in doing this, he was usurping congressional authority. Congress, and the country, would not stand for that.

Congress watched something else as well. That fall Mississippi, Georgia, Texas, South Carolina, Florida called constitutional conventions and, in every case, passed black codes that were merely a rewording of the old slave codes. The only rights they permitted the Negro were legal marriage, the right to hold property, the right to sue or be sued. For the rest: he could rent property or houses only in restricted areas; if he quit work he could be arrested and sent to the house of correction for a year; his freedom of movement was hedged about by vagrancy laws which carried penalties of hard labor or long imprisonment.

Many times colored soldiers, mustered out only a few hours, were arrested as vagrants. In some states any white man, whether authorized or not, might arrest a Negro, and in all Southern states no Negro, unless he was a soldier, could own or carry firearms. Curfew laws were established, making a Negro liable to arrest if found on the streets without a pass from his employer.

The sum of it all was clarified when certain states merely substituted "Negro" for "slave" and adopted their old slave codes.

In Tennessee and North Carolina Negroes called conventions to protest these dangers. In South Carolina and Georgia they gathered together to resist the black codes and in South Carolina they urged that "universal free education" should be provided for white children as well as Negro, that "every citizen without regard to race, descent or color" should have "equal political rights." These were conventions of black men, organized by them, in which no white men took part.

Stevens, meanwhile, was trying by every means in his power to impress the North with the fact that "more than $2,000,000,000 worth of property belonging to the United States, confiscated not as rebel but as enemy property, has been given back to enrich traitors."

Small landowners, he insisted, should hold their land, but the great landowners, "the leading rebels," should lose their property in forty acre tracts to the freedmen. The rest should be sold to pay the debts of the war.

Thus the former slaves would be cared for, the leaders of the rebellion would pay for the war, and the national debt would be taken from about the necks of the people —"yet nine-tenths of the Southerners would remain untouched."

Stevens knew that the strength of a new South lay with landowning, small farmers, independent freedmen. And so did the old South know this. "Without confiscation [that is, the assignment of land to small farmers, Negro and white]," wrote an Alabama editor, "the results of Negro suffrage will slip through their fingers."

This was a fundamental truth, for in an agricultural part of the country, landless men were without economic or political security. "Forty acres and a mule" became a slogan that every small farmer could understand.

Johnson was caught between his natural sympathies with the South and his respect for the rising Northern power of stocks, bonds, railroads, and industries. But this new North had no more sympathy for the Negro and the poor white than had the old slave masters.

The financial and industrial giant of the North, of which Johnson was the willing or unwilling servant, was concerned only with pacifying a section of the country that could yield great profits to investors. Northern capital was already making vast inroads in the South, and complete economic domination was only a matter of time.

This Northern giant considered the Negro's demand for land as a blow at the sanctity of property—land could not simply be taken from one man and given to another. This was too revolutionary a thought, and if the Negro's place in society was to be accomplished at such a shocking price—and at the price of endangering Northern investments in the South—then the Negro must look out.

"Hold the antislavery societies together," Sumner sent out warning. "The crisis is grave."

Congress, reassembling in December, saw the Vice President of the Confederacy, four Confederate generals, six Confederate Cabinet members, and fifty-eight Confederate congressmen present themselves as representatives. They based their claims to seats upon Johnson's Reconstruction plans.

Congress still rejected Johnson's right to make terms with the Confederacy, claiming that this right belonged to Congress alone. The Southerners were not seated. All winter a fight rocked back and forth. The House, more democratic than the Senate, gave the vote to the Negroes of the District of Columbia, only to have the Senate kill the resolution. Yet the two houses passed a bill giving those forty acres and the mules to the freedmen. Johnson vetoed it.

Round and round the violent carousel went . . . a white man's government . . . equality for all . . . new techniques to restore the old ways of the South . . . Johnson saying, "Damn the Negro, let's get business started!"

Stevens answered all this in his own way: "This is not a white man's government . . . this is Man's government, the government of all men alike."

Garrison found no surprise in these events. Nor did the Negro leaders of the North who were no men's dupes when it came to their own demands. Garrison had put great hope in Johnson, but he was beginning to put greater and more bitter hope in Grant's officers and men, who were still acting as an army of occupation in the old slavelands, keeping order, enforcing laws; and he put his greatest hope in the growing opposition in the North to the readmission to Congress of Confederate men and points of view.

Sumner and Stevens drove through a Civil Rights Bill in 1866. Johnson vetoed it.

This second veto disturbed many friends of Johnson. The veto was promptly overridden and Congress, in a fighting frame of mind, determined to challenge any further action of Johnson.

When the Freedmen's Bureau Bill, guaranteeing certain protections to the Negro, was presented for a second time, it rapidly passed House and Senate, and was as rapidly vetoed. Without debate, the veto was set aside, and another forward step was taken.

So the bitter fight rolled on. In the South, the friends of the Negro—Northern teachers and church groups, Union officers, former fugitive slaves, coming to the South—tried to create a living answer by encouraging some human dignity and hope. They sent urgent messages that a Fourteenth Amendment was imperative —there could be no settlement, North or South, no lasting peace, until the status of the free Negro was fixed by law.

A subtle change was taking place among Northern businessmen. Northern capital began to see the advantage of Negro suffrage. Perhaps through the Negro their hold on the South could be made permanent. An educated, independent Negro—four and a half million of him—would be a buyer of Northern goods.

A Fourteenth Amendment became suddenly as important to businessmen as had the Emancipation Proclamation to the abolitionist.

Neither Stevens nor Sumner, nor the more militant abolitionists, cared for the amendment as it was finally passed. They tried by every device to make it a clear-cut statement of citizenship rights, voting privileges, and all the guarantees assured to the whites. But they did not succeed.

In the Fourteenth Amendment the Negro was simply declared a citizen, but no mention was made of his rights as a voter; no clarification was offered of the ambiguous (to a Negro in the South) phrase that made his life, liberty, and property subject to the "due process of law." Stevens, who knew that he was dying, made one final and urgent plea for full citizenship.

The Fourteenth Amendment was ratified in nearly half the Northern states before the new Congress assembled in 1867 and rejected in all the Southern states. This was enough to show that the South, which Johnson was so eager to have back in the Union on any terms, was refusing to guarantee the free status of the Negro.

Already white-robed bands, calling themselves Ku Klux Klans, were terrorizing Negroes by day and night. Negroes, in turn, were seizing tracts of land and arming themselves to hold the land and to resist the night raiders. And Johnson was refusing all legal means of relief.

Rumor said that Johnson and the South were planning a revolt. The sweep back toward Civil War seemed obvious to the clumsiest politician, for all this appalling chaos could lead only to ruin. The radicals in Congress decided that the power that Johnson had assumed must be stripped from him before it was too late. The first move toward impeachment was made.

Stevens and Sumner had Congress with them now.

Three bills were passed in rapid succession to limit Johnson's power, and then the most important bill of all, putting the Reconstruction program into the hands of Congress, was passed.

This provided, among other things, for a constitutional government in Southern states that would ratify the Fourteenth Amendment. In this way, the amendment at last became law in 1868.

Thus into the South came that decade which has been considered one of the most degrading periods of American history. Let us see it by the facts, not the emotions.

19

THE period of Black Reconstruction has been called a carnival of corruption, a bitter revenge of slaves against masters. It was, indeed, a wild, unfettered period; but it was also a slow, painful effort to establish a new and untried way of life, a government by the majority, black and white.

In every state of the South new legislatures were now made up of the elected, and the elected were black men and white men and many were linked together by poverty. It was charged that they passed laws of revenge. The truth is, they secured legal rights for whites as well as for blacks. They argued for equal protection for all classes.

It was charged that most were ignorant and vicious, that the legislatures were conducted as though delinquent children had taken over. The truth is that, although many legislators had no education, although many trusted to the advice of friends who misled them, although some of them accepted bribes or sold their votes, although there was singing and noise in legislative assemblies, yet all of them demanded protection for the insane, the deaf, the dumb, the blind, the sick, the poor —the first social legislation in the South.

It was charged that they were bone-lazy and would not work. The truth is that by the end of these ten years the agricultural life of the South had been restored above the prewar level. Why, then, has the story of Reconstruction been told in terms of almost constant mockery and disgust?

The bitter fact is that Reconstruction was forced to prove itself at a time when national corruption and thievery in high places was a well-known scandal. It was forced to justify itself in a section of the country that had been torn by war and hardened by two hundred years of a ruthless philosophy which said that these same black men and poor white men were less than trash.

The truth is that some of these black men and poor white men were idealists, some opportunists, many profoundly ignorant, but all were agreed on the need for universal suffrage and the right to work as free men.

Had it been possible to enforce fully their legislation, a society, politically and socially advanced, might have been brought into existence.

White teachers, freedmen's agents, preachers (as well as a large number of dishonest men come to steal whatever they could lay their hands on) put their belongings into carpet bags and joined the rush to the South.

Schools were set up where reading, writing, cooking, sewing, new agricultural methods were taught. Many of the Negroes who returned to teach in these schools were veterans of the Underground Railroad.

Within the South, articulate and unprejudiced whites showed a desire to cooperate, even though it meant being called "scalawag" by the old slave masters. That many of these whites joined themselves to the Negro not from love of the Negro but because they feared the power of the planters cannot be denied. But they chose a course—whatever their reasons—that had some hope for the future.

Johnson retaliated by extending a full pardon to the Confederates and he advised his Southern friends to put a stop to the distribution of land by hurrying enjoinment suits as fast as possible. He believed this would halt congressional reconstruction.

But the courts refused to act on the enjoinment suits. To the old slave master, this left only one alternative: *intimidate and control the Negro.*

The Klan was spreading throughout the South. The Reconstructionists attempted to meet the terror by forming Union Leagues of Negroes and whites. Although women belonged to these Leagues, it was the men who drilled and formed the Negro militia. When the Klan and the League met, head on, violence followed. But the primary purpose of the League was cooperation between blacks and whites. They met to-

196

gether, they paraded together, they shouted the same slogan: *Bread, Wages, and Schools.*

That autumn elections were held and conventions formed to set up new constitutions for the states. In South Carolina, land distribution, the plight of the itinerant worker, race and color discrimination, and the right of women to vote were all debated and acted upon. The judicial system was to be enlarged, judges were to be elected instead of appointed, and mixed juries were provided. Imprisonment for debt was abolished, and black and white were allowed to vote without property qualifications.

The first governor in South Carolina, under this constitution, was an honest but weak Northerner named Scott. The second governor was Franklin Moses, Jr., a well-born South Carolinian who had, in fact, helped pull down the flag at Fort Sumter. He was now willing to go with the future as long as it benefited him.

The first secretary of state was Francis Cardozo, a man of Negro, Jewish, and Indian heritage, educated at the University of Glasgow and in London. Other Negroes holding office were Robert Elliot, who had been educated at Eton; Richard Cain, a bishop in the Methodist Church and editor of the most influential Negro paper in South Carolina; and Robert Smalls, who had piloted vessels in the Union navy.

Southern conservatives charged that this constitution was the work of sixty ignorant and depraved Negroes and of fifty white men "outcasts of Northern society and Southern renegades."

Certainly there were many raw field hands voting in this convention. There was much laughter and noise and many feet on the desks. But there was also an earnest purpose born of a conviction—instilled by some of the "carpetbaggers"—that democracy was meant to include black and white, rich and poor.

In varying degrees, the same situation was duplicated in all the Southern states as new constitutions were drawn up and the government passed to the governed.

The conservative whites never gave up the fight. Their outrage ran too deep. When public funds were dispensed with a careless zeal, they raised the cry of thievery. When former slaves stood up in the legislative halls and stumbled through a resolution to the encouraging shouts and songs of their friends, they exhausted themselves with scorn. And they laid long plans for the future.

As a beginning they tried to separate the poor whites from the Negroes by the persistent argument "we want this state to be white, ruled by whites, for whites."

In the chaotic politics of these years, only a few things were ironclad and positive to Northern businessmen: the march of Northern industrialism must be unhampered, rugged individualism and skyrocketing fortunes must be accepted as the moral principles of the day. Johnson suddenly represented an outworn form of conservatism, therefore Johnson was in sudden disgrace with those supporters who had defended him most zealously. This abruptly turned the contest between Congress and the President into a contest between autocracy and democracy, in a way that neither Stevens nor Sumner desired.

When Johnson defied the Tenure of Office Act (which said that the President could not dismiss any officeholder who had been approved by Congress, unless Congress gave its consent), impeachment finally came to a head.

By one vote, Johnson escaped, but his power was broken. Although Johnson had never talked of himself as a Republican, he stood as a Republican President, and the party suffered greatly. Northern industrialists knew that, if the Democrats won the next election, the gates of the South would be slammed against them. A strong Republican MUST be nominated to stop the rising Democratic tide and wipe out the stain of Johnson. General U. S. Grant, the hero, was selected.

Grant was elected.

When Congress gathered again, its first action was to pass the necessary resolutions for the Fifteenth Amendment which gave to all citizens, irrespective of race, color, or previous condition of servitude, the right to vote.

Stevens was not there to direct the fight, for he had died during the summer. Now he lay in a Negro burying ground, the inscription he had written carved above his head:

I repose in this quiet and secluded place, not for any natural preference for solitude, but finding other cemeteries limited as to race by charter rules,

I have chosen this that I might illustrate in my death the principles I advocated through a long life, the Equality of Man before his Creator.

But Sumner was on hand, and before galleries tense and strained with colored and white listeners, the Fifteenth Amendment was shouted through.

Here was the real triumph of abolition. Here was the end of that immemorial story. In March, 1870, the Fifteenth Amendment, giving to the Negro the right to vote, became a law, and the Negro stood up, a citizen before the world.

With celebrations and cries of joy, the antislavery societies declared their work was ended. The tears, the shouting and the speeches swept over the North and into the South. This time Garrison agreed. He was in demand from Vicksburg to Boston to set the seal on his great triumph of democracy.

In Cincinnati, before a meeting of white and colored friends who crowded every inch of the hall, Levi Coffin announced that the stock of the Underground Railroad had collapsed, the business been ruined, the road closed. To wild and joyous applause, he offered his resignation as "president."

How could anyone believe that, by every law and process of democracy, the rights of the Negro had not now been protected for all time to come? Such golden days . . . such clouds gathering on the horizon.

20

LONG ago the friends of the Negro in Congress had seen the need for education before the vote was given. But the wave of terror which followed the war had left no alternative: voting could not wait for education.

So the Negroes' plight was a bitter one. Those with no education often trusted people whom they believed to be their friends—but were not their friends.

Treachery and deceit, hunger and fear were all around. Only deep moral convictions and a hard driving program of reform would be strong enough to cut through this terrible refuse. In all the states where the Negro vote was heaviest, reform movements were undertaken.

In South Carolina, the Negro leaders, Cardozo,

Smalls, Elliot, set themselves against Governor Moses and drew up the charges against his misuse of funds. In Louisiana, the Negro lieutenant governor, Dunn, led a revolt within the Republican convention of 1870 against the public thefts of Governor Wermoth, but Wermoth weathered the storm.

Efforts were made to split the Negro from his faith in the Republican Party. In spite of all his disappointments, this was not successful. The next strategy was to concentrate upon the poor whites and try to persuade them of the old slogan that white men should stick together. With guns and midnight visits, the hooded Klan enforced this point of view.

When the congressional investigation of Klan terror was published in 1871 and 1872, it carried a long list of assorted violence. The Klan retorted that it acted only against Republicans, or against men who talked too much, or against Negroes who had insisted on being landowners or had tried to hold elections.

The army had little control over the remote country places, where most of the Klan's activities were confined. In Texas, where the army could keep only a token discipline, General Sheridan summed up the situation angrily: "If I owned both hell and Texas, I'd rent Texas and live in hell."

The Negroes struggled to consolidate their power and to defend themselves against their sea of enemies. Huge state debts were necessary to build public schoolhouses, asylums, poorhouses—all largely unknown in the prewar South. This swelled the charges of money recklessly spent. Paper inflation also helped this charge, but paper inflation was necessary because the credit for certain reconstructed states was held by New York bankers whose association with the planters made them refuse loans or credit to the "black" legislators.

President Grant appealed for laws against the Klan, laws which could also make the Fourteenth and Fifteenth amendments workable. Congress gave him extraordinary powers to deal with the situation, but the military force was inadequate and, even sadder, so corrupted by the easy money lying about that it was without heart for its duty.

The outrages continued with scarcely a break. Those arrested were freed, and a Republican governor was impeached because he had called out the militia against the Klan. At the end of the year, the special powers of the President expired, and Congress did not renew them.

Scandals were rocking the Republican Party, voters were growing restless. "Reform" was essential. A well-planned program of reform was offered to the voters that election year of 1872. The program called for new land values in the West, lower rates for railroads; in the East, assurances that businessmen would run the government and protect securities and investments; in the South a return of leadership to the men of property.

The Southern planters now rolled all their charges into one: Northern carpetbaggers (and the army was lumped in with them) were responsible for all the ills of the South. Get them out while we are still friends, said the Southern planters, and we will not interfere with Northern investments.

If the army of occupation was withdrawn, this would be a clear sign of friendliness to the planters. The Reconstruction legislators, although still controlling the administration of the South, were naive men, in no way prepared to meet a partnership of Northern and Southern experts. And, at the moment that friendliness was agreed on by the landowners of the South and the businessmen of the North, the future was settled.

Sumner did what he could. He now fought a courageous battle for civil rights, a fight he had carried with him since the Fourteenth Amendment had failed to prevent discrimination in railroads, in schools, in churches, in amusement places, on juries, even in cemeteries. He used every strategy he knew to attach his civil rights bill to other bills, and he failed sometimes by only a single vote. At last he was worn out.

Three colored men stood with congressional friends around his bed as he lay dying and heard his last hoarse plea, "You must take care of the civil rights bill—my bill, the civil rights bill—don't let it fail!"

But all such things were set for failure now. When the Republican Party split in 1872 and the Democrats gained their first congressional majority in twenty years, the end of Reconstruction was near.

Reform was still a great word, but reform crashed

against the panic of 1873. Many citizens decided that only the men who knew how to rule could stem the panic. In county after county in the South, the Democrats won.

Republicans in the South refused to give up their seats, claiming that the election had been won by all kinds of fraud. In Arkansas dual governments, one Democratic, one Republican, were set up. In Mississippi, Grant objected to the "violent revolution" which made a farce of the election, but Congress upheld the Democratic claimants, and the White League—as the Klan was called in Mississippi—patrolled the streets of Vicksburg.

Everywhere the Republican split left the Negroes standing alone while their white allies took refuge in the Democratic camp.

The 1875 elections were a sheer terror. In Clinton, Mississippi, fifteen hundred Negroes and a hundred whites, gathered at a Republican barbecue, were fired on by mobs brought down on special trains, and fifty Negroes were killed.

The governor called for presidential interference, but Grant refused to act. The state had to restore its own peace. The Negro militias were dissolved with the understanding that the Democrats would allow the Negroes to vote. But Negroes were shot down in the streets, dragged from their homes, kept from the polls. The Republican governor and lieutenant governor were made to resign and were then driven from the state.

"Mississippi is governed today by officials chosen through fraud and violence such as would scarcely be credited to savages," Grant observed bitterly, but he did nothing about it.

The new governor, chosen by the planters, soon absconded with $316,000.

In South Carolina and Louisiana the same technique was used: a split, the riding of hooded men, dual governments, and then, under the compliant shudders of the North, the full triumph of the planters.

"Every Democrat must feel honor bound to control the votes of at least one Negro, by intimidation, purchase, keeping him away, or whatsoever. Never threaten a man individually. If he deserves to be threatened, the necessities of the time require that he should die." The man who gave these instructions won his way to the governorship of South Carolina by combining these methods with false ballots at the polls, and he consolidated his power by driving out seventeen Republicans who had been elected.

All through the South, that terrible fall of 1876, the Negroes were the victims. The Democrat, Samuel J. Tilden, and the Republican, Rutherford B. Hayes, were contesting the presidency. Tilden's electoral votes stood at 184, Hayes' at 166. Four states—South Carolina, Louisiana, Florida, and Oregon—were in doubt, but Hayes claimed them.

In this period of electoral frauds, it was a hard claim to prove. While the Senate commission tried to disen-

206

tangle the mess, and the violence of the old days roared up and down the aisles of the House, a deal took place behind the scenes. A written promise was made by Hayes's advisers that if Florida, South Carolina, and Louisiana assured him the presidency, he would promise that complete control would be returned to those states and no laws would be considered binding except the Constitution. All troops would be withdrawn, and men of property would be put in control again.

The Southern Democrats were faithful to the Republican Hayes, and he, in turn, kept his word. Florida, South Carolina, Louisiana were, by the simple expedient of withdrawing the troops, handed over to the rival governments which the planters had set up.

For a time Negro congressmen came up the long road to Washington, but for the average Negro a dream had ended. State laws began to close in on him, state laws which skillfully got around the Constitution. "Grandfather" clauses denied the vote to a man whose grandfather had been a slave. Poll-tax and educational requirements began to whittle away at his right to protest. Little was left him but remembrances of the past.

But once a man has proved that he is a man, it is difficult to force him to be a slave again. The human spirit is dauntless when it has glimpsed something of the truth.

And behind the Negro now were great memories of daring and courage and resolution. They had Denmark Vesey and Nat Turner, who had seen no strangeness in a black Messiah. They had Douglass clasping the hands of Garrison, and all the unknown friends who had sprung up, like Cadmus's teeth, from the ground. They had the disguises, the closed carriages, the gunshots along the border, and the long resolute train which chugged so silently and sent up such invisible smoke.

They had those unnamed heroes who decided in the darkness of a Southern night where the train would stop, and those other heroes who made the journeys back from freedom because they loved freedom so well. They had all the freemen and the freedmen who tried to make democracy work within the old slavelands, who had given their lives before and would have given them again.

In America, a minority had not found freedom. But this was not the end. The seeds lay deep. The fruit would grow.

Forever free . . . that was the promise, and it would be kept.

BIBLIOGRAPHY

Bancroft, Frederic. *Slave Trading in the Old South.* Baltimore: J. H. Furst, 1931.

Brawley, Benjamin G. *A Short History of the American Negro.* New York: The Macmillan Company, 1927.

Carroll, Joseph C. *Slave Insurrections in the United States, 1800–1865* Boston: Chapman & Grimes, 1938.

Catterall, Helen T. *Judicial Cases Concerning American Slavery and the Negro.* Washington: Carnegie Institute, 1929.

Coffin, Levi. *Reminiscences of Coffin, the Reported President of the Underground Railroad.* Cincinnati: n.p., 1876.

Commager, Henry Steele. *Theodore Parker.* Boston: Little, Brown & Company, 1936.

Dodd, William E. *The Cotton Kingdom.* New Haven: Yale University Press, 1919.

Douglass, Frederick. *Life and Times of Frederick Douglass, Written by Himself.* Boston: DeWolfe Fiske & Company, 1892; New York: Pathway Press, 1941.

DuBois, W. E. B. *Black Reconstruction.* New York: Harcourt, Brace & Company, 1935.

Eaton, John. *Grant, Lincoln and the Freedmen*. New York: Longmans, Green & Company, 1907.

Gaines, Francis Pendleton. *The Southern Plantation*. New York: Columbia University Press, 1924.

Garrison, Wendell Phillips and F. J. Garrison. *William Lloyd Garrison, 1805–1907; the Story of His Life Told By His Children*. Boston: Houghton Mifflin Company, 1894.

Hart, Albert Bushnell, editor. *Slavery and Abolition, 1831–1841*. (*The American Nation: A History*, Vol. XVI.) New York: Harper & Brothers, 1906.

Helper, Hinton Rowan. *The Impending Crisis in the South: How to Meet It*. New York: Burdick Brothers, 1857.

Kemble, Frances Anne. *Journal of a Residence on a Georgian Plantation*. New York: Harper & Brothers, 1863.

May, Samuel. *Some Recollections of Our Anti-Slavery Conflict*. Boston: Fields, Osgood & Company, 1869.

Miller, Alphonse B. *Thaddeus Stevens*. New York: Harper & Brothers, 1939.

Olmsted, Frederick Law. *The Cotton Kingdom* (originally published 1861). Edited, with an Introduction, by Arthur M. Schlesinger. New York: Alfred A. Knopf, Inc., 1953.

Ross, Alexander M. *Recollections and Experiences of an Abolitionist; from 1855 to 1865*. Toronto: Roswell & Hutchinson, 1875.

Sandburg, Carl. *Abraham Lincoln: The Prairie Years* and *The War Years*. New York: Harcourt, Brace & Company, 1926–1939.

Siebert, Wilbur H. *The Underground Railroad from*

Slavery to Freedom. New York: The Macmillan Company, 1898.

Sinclair, Upton. *Manassas; a Novel of the War*. New York: The Macmillan Company, 1904.

Still, William. *The Underground Railroad. A Record of Facts, Authentic Narratives, Letters, etc*. Philadelphia: Porter & Coates, 1872.

Stowe, Harriet Beecher. *Uncle Tom's Cabin; or Life among the Lowly*. 2 vols. Boston: John P. Jewett & Company, 1852.

————. *A Key to Uncle Tom's Cabin*. Boston: John P. Jewett & Company, 1853.

Tatum, Georgia Lee. *Disloyalty in the Confederacy*. Chapel Hill: University of North Carolina Press, 1934.

Villard, Oswald Garrison. *John Brown, 1800–1859; a Biography Fifty Years After*. Boston: Houghton Mifflin Company, 1910.

Wiley, Bell Irvin. *Southern Negroes, 1861–1865*. New Haven: Yale University Press, 1938.

Wilson, Henry. *History of the Rise and Fall of the Slave Power in America*. Boston: J. R. Osgood & Company, 1872–1874.

Woodson, Carter G. *The Negro in Our History*. Washington: The Associated Publishers, Inc., 1927.

INDEX

abolitionism (*see also* anti-slavery), 27-28
  force, use of, 143-145
  growth of, 47, 61-62, 66, 76
  principles of, 67-68, 89
abolitionists:
  attacks on, 99-101
  and Lincoln, 147, 149-150, 156, 158, 159, 160, 167, 180
  and moderation, 61-63, 133, 138, 143
  Northern opposition to, 47-52, 54, 55-57, 100
  and political parties, 66-69, 138
Adams, John Quincy, 28, 62, 76
agriculture, Southern, 7
Aldridge, Ira, 72
Alton, Ill., riot, 65
American Antislavery Society, split in, 69
Anderson, Robert, Major, 152, 182
Anthony, Susan B., 68, 121
Antietam, battle of, 166
antislavery (*see also* abolition-ism), 27
  and politics, 66-69, 76
  propaganda of, 21, 26, 30, 35-37, 45, 52-53, 118-120, 130
  Southern support for, 41, 68, 112-114, 148, 173
  split in, 69, 92-93

antislavery societies, 49, 57
Arkansas, dual government, 205
army of occupation, 190, 202, 203, 204, 207

"barnburners," 94
Birney, James, 69
Black Codes, 187
Black Laws, 95
Black Prophet, 38
Black Reconstruction, 194-198, 201-207
"Blood Money," 104
border states, 158, 160, 164, 166, 171
Boston, 12, 55-57
Boston Female Antislavery Society, 55
boycott of slave products, 80-81
Breckinridge, John C., 148
Bremer, Fredrika, 41
British emancipation, 38
Brooks, Preston, 131
Brown, Henry Box, 96-98
Brown, John, 11, 131-132, 143-145
Brown, William Wells, 72
Buchanan, James, 132, 133, 138, 141, 147, 151, 152
Burns, Anthony, 125-128
businessmen, Northern:
  antislavery attitude of, 51, 53, 57, 108, 114-115, 117, 125
  freedmen, attitude toward, 189, 191

212

213

216

217

ABOUT THE AUTHOR

Henrietta Buckmaster lives in New York, where she devotes her time to writing. She is the author of many books and magazine articles. One of her chief interests is the story of slavery in the United States, and out of this interest came *Flight to Freedom*. Miss Buckmaster feels that the more we know about our history, the better we will be able to solve our problems. She has received a number of awards and fellowships for her books, most of which have been translated into several languages.

Miss Buckmaster's family came from the South; but she was born in Cleveland, Ohio, and educated in New York at the Friends School and the Brearley School. She has traveled widely throughout the United States and Europe.